le corbusier

le corbusier

Carlo Cresti

Hamlyn

London   New York   Sydney   Toronto

twentieth–century masters
General editors: H. L. Jaffé and A. Busignani

© Copyright in the text Sadea/Sansoni, Florence 1969
© Copyright in the illustrations SPADEM Paris 1969
© Copyright this edition The Hamlyn Publishing Group Limited 1970
London · New York · Sydney · Toronto
Hamlyn House, Feltham, Middlesex, England
ISBN 0 600 35403 2

Colour lithography: Zincotipia Moderna, Florence
Printing and binding: Cox and Wyman Limited
London, Fakenham and Reading

Distributed in the United States of America by Crown Publishers Inc.

contents

List of colour plates

List of black-and-white illustrations

Architecture is conditioned by the
spirit of an epoch, and the spirit
of an epoch is made up of the depth
of history, the idea of the present
and discernment of the future.

The first of Le Corbusier's projects to show the unmistakable signs of a premeditated statement of principle and method is the framework for the Dom-Ino house of 1914. This is so fundamentally mature at its first appearance that one cannot believe there were no precedents. His early works (the two villas of La Chaux-de-Fonds and the project for artists' studios of 1910) hardly qualify as precedents since they do not have the clarity of conceptual planning which distinguishes the Dom-Ino house.

'*L'intuition agit par éclairs inattendus*' are the opening words of the presentation of the Dom-Ino project in the *Œuvre complete* 1910–29. This self-sufficient structure, appearing like some extraordinary gift of fate may very well seem a 'sudden flash of inspiration' to anyone who does not bother to inquire into the origins of the circumstances which brought about the amazing difference between the villas of La Chaux-de-Fonds and the Dom-Ino house.

By examining the various ideologies and their application in architecture, which were characteristic of the restless state of European culture between the beginning of the century and the First World War, one can retrace in some detail the various opportunities Le Corbusier had for instruction and the contacts he made, which were to influence his later work and which doubtless played a part in furthering the vocational principles of Le Corbusier's style.

Such an investigation is not intended to be a reappraisal of values nor an attempt to diminish merit but aims to describe objectively all the elements which contribute to logical development in the technological field, bearing in mind Quatremere de Quincy's statement that 'the art of constructing properly stems from pre-existing seed. Everything must have an antecedent; nothing whatever comes from nothing, and this must be applied to all man's inventions.'[1] 'Iconographically every element of rationalist architecture had reached a concrete conclusion.'[2] Before 1914 many people had contributed to the affirmation of this new reality. Perret was the first to find 'new architectural means in the unexplored potential of ferro-concrete'[3] and in the house in rue Franklin he clearly anticipated the figurative possibilities of a visible structure. Behrens and Gropius had stressed and extolled the poetry of steel and large areas of glass in their industrial buildings; Garnier in his *cité industrielle* had codified the technical principles of modern town-planning and finally Loos had adopted in the Steiner house 'the complete elimination of every non-structural element'.[4]

'Intuition works in sudden flashes'

1 Quatremère de Quincy, *Dictionnaire Historique de l'Architecture*, Paris, 1832.
2 B. Zevi, *Storia dell'Architettura Moderna*, Chapter III: *I Maestri del periodo razionalista*.
3 S. Giedion. *Space, Time and Architecture*, Harvard University Press, 1967. Chapter IV.
4 L. Benevolo, *Storia dell'Architettura Moderna*, Vol. I, Chapter IX: Adolf Loos.

Le Corbusier, like a sensitive seismograph, has the not inconsiderable distinction of bringing into the open what was already inherent in the European cultural scene and of outlining it in its new role of 'movement', by collecting together the best features and presenting them in a strict vocabulary.

One should therefore examine these features, considering them as the conscious confirmation of existing facts, and recognising that they have a valuable contribution to make, which is not just the possibility of the superficial appropriation of an existing language, nor does it merely offer scope for imitation.

Adolf Loos and the Viennese Secession

Le Corbusier first came into contact with the environment of the Viennese Secession in 1907. Although he came to know Hoffman, who was at that time engaged on the construction of the Stoclet palace, he was definitely attracted by the personality of Adolf Loos who was working on the edge of cultural officialdom.

When Loos returned from his 'purifying' voyage to the United States,[5] 'he took advantage of his experience of rationalist architecture, unknown in the Europe of 1880–90, and avoided being swept up by the *Art Nouveau* movement, which was the set path for the culture of the old continent'.[6] Liberated from academic and conformist backwash, he saw 'the spirit of Potemkin'[7] hovering over the Viennese architecture of the Ringstrasse; Vienna was for him the 'city of deceptive mirages',[8] a city where decorative gilding belied the reality of social classes.

Closer in his moral severity to the ideology of Munch (whose graphic work he must certainly have admired in the 1904 exhibition in Vienna) than to the 'gilded' escapism of Klimt, Loos wanted to liberate the banal, neglected things of everyday life from the suffocating aesthetic flattery of the *Jugendstil*. To that end he urged 'the description of how birth and death, how the cries of pain of a son hurt in an accident, how a mother's dying gasps and the last thoughts of a daughter who wants to take her own life happen and are portrayed in Olbrich's bedroom'.[9] Just as Munch challenged the hypocrisy of the bourgeoisie and denounced its most secret ancestral taboos, so Loos fought the sensual exhibitionism of Klimt's ornamentation, for him a symbol of the aesthetic inflation which was poisoning society.

In direct opposition to the Secessionist idea of the integral work of art, Loos maintained that 'the evolution of culture is synonymous with the exclusion of ornament from useful objects'.[10] Adhering to this belief, he wrote the essay *Ornament and Crime* in 1908 as a reply to Hoffman's Stoclet palace (although Hoffman was certainly not the artist most 'corrupted' by ornament in the circle of the Viennese Secession). Finally, in 1910, he built the Steiner house which was to be the archetype of European rationalist architecture. In contrast to the exuberant, overstylised details which belie the mass to emphasise the surface, Loos stressed the volumetric purity of the edifice, the poetry of function exalted to spatial definition. Reliving in European terms the American spatial experience, Loos concentrated all his interest and research on the inside of the dwelling. He brought it to life with rhythm and spatial interpenetrations which are defined and motivated, the logical result of human actions and various psychological situations. He confined his details to these internal paths of tension in answer to precise functions. This interior equilibrium, controlled by a hierarchy of spaces, is reiterated outside only in the volumetric articulation of masses (for example the three projecting parallelepipids which, by their interlocking give added

5 In 1893 Loos visited the United States for the first time and his contact with the American environment and especially his study of the architecture of the School of Chicago played a decisive part in his cultural education.
6 B. Zevi, op. cit., Chapter II. *La prima età dell'architettura moderna.*
7 A. Loos, *Die potemkinsche, Stadt, Ver Sacrum,* anno I, July, 1898.
8 A. Loos, op. cit.
9 A. Loos, *Sämtliche Schriften.* Vienna, 1962. Vol. I. Quoted in W. Hofman, *Klimt e la secessione viennese* 'Arte Moderna', No. 19, Volume 3, Milan, 1967.
10 A. Loos, *Ornament und verbrechen;* the essay was written in 1908, translated into French and published in the second number of the review *L'Esprit Nouveau.*

importance to the mass of the Steiner house; as with the motif of the graded terraces of the Scheu house). This volumetric purity is expressed even more clearly by the severe simplicity of the elevations. Above the rudimentary surface supports are inserted the windows, arranged in a reticulated pattern and reduced to the bare essentials for the necessary intake of light and air. In both the Steiner and the Scheu houses one can sense the anguished search for the essence of things, the preoccupation with achieving an immediate truth, a desire to be scrupulously true to the actions of life. It was almost as though Loos anticipated the confusion which was to come after the Sarajevo assassination, troubling Europe and changing, with tragic results, all the decorative trivialities and formal flattery of a happy-go-lucky society.

Le Corbusier understood intuitively the historical maturity of these trends and absorbed them naturally, as he tended to regard architectural problems from the same ideological standpoint as Loos.

A quotation from Le Corbusier's homage to Loos of 1931 supports this view: 'Loos appeared suddenly in the midst of our architectural preoccupation with a marvellous article published in 1908, *Ornament and Crime*. We had come to the end of a sentimental period, we had renewed contact with nature and had at last completely mastered the new techniques (construction in steel and concrete, new machines, new materials). All this meant a decisive break with the past, which the Academies were keeping alive artificially, and at the same time it meant impatient preparation for the future. Loos swept beneath our feet, and made a clean break – Homeric, accurate, philosophical and lyrical. In this way Loos influenced our architectural future.'[11]

In the drawings he made while very young at L'Eplattenier's school Le Corbusier had shown his first real interest in the wavy and flame-like line. In the language of *Art Nouveau* this motif exhausts its own potential in a magic labyrinth of shining gold, and decoration becomes an end in itself, but for Le Corbusier it becomes a constructive element, which, even in its decorative meanderings evokes volumes rather than surfaces; the line of a sculptor rather than a painter. Even looking at the preparatory drawings for an engraving, studies of roots and plants, or at the sketch of the now famous watch exhibited at the International Exhibition of Decorative Art at Turin in 1902, one has to admit that the few strokes outlining the overlapping planes in these drawings convey the impression of a third dimension.

This spontaneous tendency to achieve linear simplicity, the scant attention to the attractions of decoration (as an end in itself), and the desire to rationalise things were all derived from L'Eplattenier's teachings[12] and formed the basis of Le Corbusier's education, to which Loos's themes were readily attractive.

The experience Le Corbusier gained from his contact with Perret (1908–9) lay in the new possibilities offered by building in reinforced concrete, which Perret was using at that time. In the house in rue Franklin (1903) the walls were reduced to partitions, allowing a flexible treatment of the ground plan which led the way for the triumph of the 'free plan'. Moreover, they could be entirely replaced with thin glass surfaces, as was demonstrated soon after in the façade of the garage in rue Ponthieu (1905).

This event was another step (immediately following Horta's contribution[13] of 1897) in the slow European evolution towards the definition of continuous horizontal fenestration.[14] Adopted subsequently by Poelzig in

Industrialisation of the architectural product

11 Le Corbusier, *Hommage à Adolf Loos*, Paris, 1931.
12 Maurice Besset (*Le Corbusier* in *Enciclopedia Universale dell'Arte*, VIII) puts forward the hypothesis that Le Corbusier knew of the decorative rationalism of the École de Nancy (Prouve, Sourian) through L'Eplattenier's teaching.
13 B. Zevi, op. cit., Chapter III.
14 Horizontal fenestration has become with time one of the distinctive external marks of European rationalist architecture. It is perhaps important, therefore, to examine the various contributions made to its structural evolution by the main architects of the period. One must not forget, however, that several years before the end of the nineteenth century this façade element had already been adopted in the average American building as a logical result of steel structuring and was particularly well-defined in the work of architects of the School of Chicago. To list a few quick examples among others are the Leiter Building by W. Le Baron Jenney of 1879; the Daily Times Building of 1884, the Tacoma building and the Marquette Building of Halaberd and Roche of 1888 and 1894 respectively,

the offices of Breslau (1910) and by Gropius[15] in the Fagus factory (1911), through Le Corbusier it was to reach its most perfect realisation, first in the façade of the villa at Garches (1927) and then in the villa Savoye (1928–30).

In Behrens's studio, where he worked in Berlin in 1910, rather than learning lessons of form or content, young Le Corbusier went straight to the heart of the burning controversy of the moment, the problems of the industrialisation of architecture. He was intrigued by Behrens's concept of mass-production (which represents the ideological liberation of the *Deutscher Werkbund* from the heritage of Morris's inspiration) as a hypothesis for meeting the needs of a changing social structure, and found it convincing.

The German architect's Turbine factory (1909–11) and his *Werkbund* pavilion in Cologne (1914) were still to come, but they would certainly not have been of such stimulating inspiration. Behrens's figurative repertoire, formed at Darmstadt under the influence of Olbrich, is based on a monumentality which destroys the concentration of rational themes. This fundamental and recurrent aspect of Behrens's work can only have had an indifferent effect on someone like Le Corbusier, and was not followed up by him later.

Instead, with his instinctively questioning approach, Le Corbusier discovered elements which were eventually to enrich his make-up in the work of the independent Tony Garnier whom he had occasion to meet in 1908 in Lyons. Garnier, who had a classically-based cultural background, adopted a policy of realistic action, being intent on solving social problems by town-planning schemes over wide areas. His *cité industrielle*[16] is an 'attempt to adapt town-planning structures to the demands of a society which, because of industrialisation is headed towards a redistribution of property and a uniformity of needs';[17] it is the 'spectacular preview of the rational city: almost all the buildings are of reinforced concrete with columns and projecting roofs poised in space, and schools have classrooms appearing from the outside like open spaces and covered terraces . . .'[18]

Le Corbusier's perceptive understanding of contemporary situations meant that he supported Garnier's point of view and must have examined in detail the principles behind the project: a clear-cut division between the various urban functions with planning for future expansion, open construction to avoid the monotony of traditional straight lines, pedestrian paths independent of the streets, green areas set aside for the community. Finally, besides laying down sanitary standards, he defined the type of assistance to be given by the public administration in the direction of the new town-planning system: 'In search of arrangements which best satisfy the physical and moral needs of the individual, we have been led to establish rules for each sector . . . and we have assumed those social developments to have already taken place which would guarantee a normal application of these regulations, which present laws would not permit. We have therefore assumed that the administration would have free disposal of the land and that it is its responsibility to make provisions for water, bread, meat, milk and medicine, given the care these products need.'[19] Rereading these statements today, one cannot help appreciating their obvious topicality and noticing their bearing on Le

15 B. Zevi, op. cit., Chapter III.
16 The project for *Une cité industrielle* was submitted by Garnier, then a student at the French Academy in Rome, in 1901 for the Grand Prix de Rome. In 1904 the plans were exhibited in Paris but the whole work was not published until 1917.
17 Giorgio Piccinato. *L'architettura contemporanea in Francia.* Chapter II: *I precorsori, Tony Garnier Auguste Perret.*
18 B. Zevi, op. cit., Chapter II.
19 Tony Garnier, *Une cité industrielle, étude pour la construction des villes,* Paris, 1939.

Burnham's Reliance building of 1894 (note the typical partitioning of the so-called Chicago window with a large fixed, central window and two side-windows which open, adopted by Gropius in his project for the Chicago Tribune competition of 1922); the Carson and Pirie stores, the Gage Building both of 1908–9 built by Sullivan, all in Chicago; the Singer Building by Ernest Flagg of 1901 in New York and the Hallidie building by Polk, 1918, at San Francisco, with its front entirely of glass heralding the epoch of the curtain-wall. It is easy to suppose that, thanks to the wide circulation and diffusion of news and pictures characteristic of the first years of our century, these Transatlantic examples must have facilitated European architects' studies in this direction to the point of limiting the originality of their results.

Corbusier's later writings, which immediately makes one think that the 'principles' of the *cité industrielle* are in real anticipation of the 'Plan of Athens' which was to come.

In addition Le Corbusier must have examined Garnier's new architectural forms (which were surprising for that time) contained in the building projects. These were so rigidly consistent with the arrangement of the imagined urban context that they offered the first complete solution at least at the planning stage to the integral relationship between architecture and town-planning. In his *Space, Time and Architecture*, Giedion shrewdly places side by side a drawing for Garnier's *cité industrielle* (1901–4)–houses of reinforced concrete with open stairways and roof-gardens–and a photograph of a building by Le Corbusier at Pessac (1925). The comparison could not be more pointed or conclusive.

Travels in Italy and Greece

It is therefore reasonable to argue that one should not think of Le Corbusier's architectural phenomena as spontaneous conception but rather as the result of a number of selected but very different contributing influences. At this point one must assess whether Le Corbusier's study of the architecture of the past during his travels in Italy, the Balkans, Greece and Turkey and the problems confronted there made any further contribution to his complex formative development.

He first visited Italy in 1906; his intensely committed approach to the 'sights' was not in order to prove the canons of harmonious proportion but because he wanted to find out what the controlling factors had been behind the successive stages of development resulting from man's conscious interventions. He lingered over the more prominent monuments of the past because in them the experiences and social content which are fostered by urban existence are more tangible and because their features were more symptomatic of things to come. This is not to say that he regarded a city as an exclusive mosaic of more legible elements which distract attention from the more obscure or isolated features, but rather as an entity which grows through spontaneous or planned intervention and which contains within it the potential of imparting an instructive message.

Faced with a work of architecture (the city being architecture on a large scale), he confronted it critically, not only from a subjective point of view which would not be enough to appreciate its true value, but also from a more objective standpoint, taking into account the many complex influences which make up architecture. Rather than a method of study as such, one should perhaps speak of 'methodical guesswork' in which he unsystematically explored issues sometimes more of a geographical nature, sometimes concerned either with form or social character, or even with special concepts jotted down impetuously and emphatically, and which, although only roughly outlined, point to a more scientific scrutiny to come.

Fig. 1   In the two sketches of Pisa, through his economic use of strokes, unencumbered by picturesque or romantic embellishments, he captures the relative positions of the different buildings and their spatial relationships. In the physical interdependence between the various masses, he grasps the importance of the pathways, contrasting them with the bulk of the Baptistery. The passage between the wall of the Camposanto and the side of the Cathedral contains for him a whole planning story which is restated on a smaller scale on the other side of the wide space surrounding the Baptistery in the corridors of the nearby city network.

The dynamic tension which the leaning of the Tower sets up between the buildings in the *piazza dei miracoli* and the logical, attendant interrelationships between the masses are seen to reappear twenty-eight years later if one compares the drawing with the rapid sketch for the competition for the Palace of the Soviets: 'one uses one's eyes . . . and draws so as to retain deep down in one's experience what is seen. Once the impression has been recorded by the pencil, it stays for good, entered, registered, inscribed for life; once written down, it is recorded for ever.'[20]

His second study tour was in 1911, 'off Eastwards . . . Prague, Danube, Serbia, Rumania, Bulgaria, Turkey (Constantinople), Asia Minor. Twenty-one days at Mount Athos . . . Athens, Acropolis six weeks. The columns of the north façade and the architrave of the Parthenon were still lying on the ground. Touching them with his fingers, caressing them, he grasps the proportions of the design. Amazement before reality has nothing in common with text-books. Here everything is a shout of inspiration, a dance in the sunlight . . . a final and supreme warning: do not believe until you have seen and measured and touched with your fingertips.'[21]

Meanwhile, between the time of his first and second journey, there had been an increasing interest in the *avant-garde* in Europe: in 1907, with his painting *Les Demoiselles d'Avignon*, Picasso had freed pictorial space from the accepted limitations of optical vision and prepared to enjoy his Cubist adventure, while Braque in his *collages* was pasting newspapers and all sorts of objects on to canvas and creating a sort of multiple space which materialises in the interaction of light and form. In 1909 Marinetti took Paris and Europe by storm with his diatribe in the columns of *Le Figaro*, full of Futurist assertions: 'the magnificence of the world is enriched with a new beauty, the beauty of speed . . . Why should we have to look backwards when we want to break through the mysterious doors of the impossible? Time and Space died yesterday. We are already living in the absolute because we have created everlasting, omnipresent speed . . .'[22]

But this controversial argument, which questioned all the accepted notions about consciousness and conscience, was expressed in terms too reactionary not to raise doubts that this new reality, a direct result of the new ideas about space, might not be found at a less absolute stage.

Despite the fact that Einstein as early as 1904 had put forward the general theory of relativity, architecture at the time was still controlled (as it is even today) by a typically three-dimensional syntax. The new concept of space could not be arrived at and achieved with untried and unduly optimistic proposals at the project level. Although Le Corbusier was familiar with the architecture which preceded Cubism and Futurism and had carefully assessed what was new in its contribution, he found that because of his lack of building experience, he had not even been able up to then to test the validity of the 'old' Euclidean (three-dimensional) space in relation to human activity. In practice, therefore, he was not ready for the new, unknown factors of Time

20 Le Corbusier, *My Work*. Translated by James Palmes, introduction by Maurice Jardot. The Architectural Press, London, 1960.
21 Le Corbusier, op. cit.
22 F. T. Marinetti, *Manifesto del futurismo*, published for the first time in French in the columns of *Le Figaro*, February 20th, 1909.

and Space which had certainly not been altogether resolved by the Cubist development. This reaction was not one of feeble resignation but that of a young man who, faced with a present which seemed further removed and more hazardous than the past, chose to seek his experience in dialectic contact with antiquity.

Travelling back through history, he made a note of the forms of the social structures where the benefits of community living brought informed progress. In one sequence of notes he set out to discover the existential constant which is the essence of architecture.

The Acropolis became an example of the uselessness of symmetries (what were Vignola and the *Prix de Rome* worth now?)[23] Le Corbusier was not concerned with the plastic values of the structures but with the interrelationship between their outer shapes. In his ground plan, attempting to reconstruct the geometric line running between the buildings and to establish their proper position, he clearly shows one offsetting another. From the Propylaeum, the Parthenon appears to the rear, a metaphysical presence, an organ which has outlived its function and which no longer has any role in the interplay of the parts of the urban network lying below.

Fig. 2

The dialogue between the buildings on the Acropolis, however, is now isolated from the rest of the world, crystallised in time up on the hill. To understand it, one should not seek to understand the arrangement of the buildings. It is enough to measure the rhythmic interplay of the spaces between the elevations—the relationship between mass and the surrounding space—to understand the reciprocal effects of the town-planning.

The walls of Byzantium, and the Tulip mosque are the focal points of different human interests, they are what has lasted of a civilisation which has changed gradually over the years, and time has only partly changed the emphasis of their function. Le Corbusier tried to fathom the successive stages grafted on to the old root and to see how far the root had fostered the development. The ground plan of the mosque is the pattern by which one can establish the relationship between the walled structure and the courtyard, the courtyard and the piazza, the piazza and the city and the city and the form of the site. In his outline drawing of the city, seen from the sea, he fixed the shape of the dome and minarets of Sta Sophia against the horizon of the Bosphorus flowing into the Black Sea, then, coming closer, brought into relief the compact mass of the Harem against the foreground of the city walls. This arrangement follows the original pattern of development where content was more important than form and the architecture is shown as having gradually spread over urban land as a result of successive operations.

The Turkish houses depicted projecting unevenly from their tight-packed base suggest that he studied the course of the wall where it intersects the

23 Le Corbusier, op. cit.

street and where it merges with it. The enclosed stretch, over which the corbels of the most protruding parts of the building meet and which ends in the clean break of the gates, provides a contrast with the openness of the street space. Where the enclosing wall is lower, allowing foliage to spill on to the street and regain a free dimension, a contact and continuity is established with the courtyard area which is emphasised by the breaking up of the line of the wall.

Le Corbusier, therefore, was not seeking any explanation of the architecture and town-planning of the past in terms of aesthetics, nor on a functional level, because function is only a limitation, even, in the long run, a distortion for the purpose of interpretive analysis.

Examining the whole question of the structure of urban organisation in a recent study, Aldo Rossi made the observation that 'an urban plan brought about by function alone is of no use beyond the fulfilment of that function. In fact, we continue to make use of elements which no longer have any function, so their significance comes to lie solely in their form. Their form is an integral part of the overall form of the city, and as one might say, an invariable feature of it.'[24] But besides form, which can also be a dangerous limitation when translated into present-day terms, Le Corbusier was looking for reality, truth, the changed logic of space as the primary condition of every act of existence. Even if the relative measurements and links between ancient architecture and its urban context could not be adapted to the new dimensions of the time, Le Corbusier was nevertheless in the powerful position of having, if only once, measured the relationship at first hand. It was definitely not a case of enlarging the scale in proportion to new requirements, nor of using it indiscriminately in just any contemporary realisations; it was rather a question of remembering that in that particular situation and within those measurements a complete living pattern was embodied. The spatial relation created a state of harmony in which man could suitably live.

'History,' as Gregotti rightly says, 'is like a beginning of awareness, ground we have to cross in order to arrive at an understanding of the structures of things but which we have to leave behind when it comes to making changes.'[25] Inevitably, though, as Bergson says, 'memory forces a thing from the past into the present'[26] and it reappears, essential to one's purpose, just when one is confronting the recurrent reality of life with plans and projects.

In the last analysis, Le Corbusier's acquaintance with the past, and his painstaking study of it gave him a basis of essential information and knowledge, not for use as a formal reference but as an introduction to planning and as a pattern of behaviour which encouraged the revaluation of existing relations and a reappraisal of the structures attributed with a mythical dimension and importance.

The spirit behind the forms

Having identified the various influences which provided a grounding and knowledge for the first phase of development of Le Corbusier's talents up to the Dom-Ino project, one ought next to examine the social and cultural stimuli which accompanied his second period of development. This next period may be described as one which developed his artistic personality and during which the figurative elements of his artistic theory became defined. One ought to assess whether these environmental pressures influenced him, and how much, and to establish by what means, if any, they were absorbed into his figurative world.

Before the war changed the face of Europe, Marinetti had once again attempted to rouse the world with the outspoken harangue of the Manifesto

24 Aldo Rossi, *L'Architettura della Città*, Padova, Marsilio, 1966. Chapter I: *Struttura dei fatti urbani.*
25 Vittorio Gregotti, *Il territorio dell'Architettura*, Milan, Feltrinelli, 1966. Part three: *Architettura e storia.*
26 Henri Bergson, *L'evoluzione creatrice*, 1906.

of Futurist Architecture.[27] But the call was scarcely heeded, partly through indifference and partly because the pamphlet was obviously the result of a hurried attempt to recover ground which had by then been lost through lack of cultural activity in Italy.[28] The architecture of the manifesto was, and still is, an architecture of words, with obvious contradictions, a superficial précis of pseudo-innovation which, while eavesdropping on the best international experiments, spurned them for the sake of a supposed revival. This was to be a revival realised by 'strokes of genius' but one which clearly hid the seed of nationalist assertion and was conditional and reactionary.[29] It is not known definitely whether Le Corbusier had occasion or not to see the Futurist manifesto, nor even if he took any interest afterwards in the other manifestoes which appeared so often and in such numbers at that time. One may suppose that if this was so, he would have reacted with the same wary detachment he had adopted towards other figurative 'isms'; typical of one who collects information and analyses its true content before discarding it.

These pictorial experiments in the field of painting (Cubism, Futurism, Suprematism) challenged the traditional concept of space (or more precisely, maintained that the depiction of static space was not enough to express the new reality of 'time' and 'speed'). Le Corbusier's diffident attitude towards them is perhaps partly explained by the fact that architectural space was already being used progressively in every direction and even in its more obscure corners was regarded as 'relative' space.[30] Space through movement which comes quite close to the concept of synchronism, was also quite usual in classical architecture, which was planned and perhaps even drawn up with reference to a fixed point. Even that space which was limited by the introduction of symmetries was, and still is, fully exploited in reality, because what appears to be immobile gains mobility through successive visual angles.

In conclusion one should realise that the phenomenon which for painting represented a decisive and explosive victory, a radical transformation, was only reflected in architecture as a partial innovation. A new architecture was already on the way so that the pictorial experiments, although stimulating, were only complementary. The new pictorial style, stripped of all decorative superfluities, brought the breaking up of mass through the overlapping and interpenetration of surfaces and volumes. The application of this new configuration from painting to architecture resulted in the replacement of symmetry by contrast and the abolition of arbitrary rhythms and basic pedantic reiteration.[31]

To appreciate the insubstantial effect of the 'isms' of the time on Le Corbusier's work, one has only to look at the projects of the period. The

27 This is not the place to discuss the controversy which developed in 1956–7 over the authenticity of Antonio Sant'Elia as a Futurist, after the discovery, by the hand of the architect, Bernasconi di Lugano, of a *Messaggio* earlier in date than the draft of the *Manifesto dell' Architettura futurista*. There is a complete bibliography on the subject in the essay by Alberto Longatti, *Antonio Sant'Elia tra decadentismo e futurismo,* published in the catalogue to the permanent exhibition of Antonio Sant'Elia, Como, 1962.
28 In this context there is an interesting extract from a letter Marinetti sent to Mac Delmarie after the controversial notices aroused against Montmartre by the manifesto in August, 1913: 'More than any other country, Italy urgently needed Futurism because it was dying of traditionalism.' (From *Archivi del Futurismo,* De Luca, Romo, 1958.)
29 Quoting from the same letter: 'we profess an ultra-violent anti-clerical and anti-socialist nationalism, and anti-traditional nationalism, which has as a basis the inexhaustible vigour of Italian blood'. (From *Archivi del Futurismo,* De Luca, Roma, 1958.)
30 The reader who has followed and understood would only have to climb the stairs of the Eiffel Tower to have an example of a dynamic-spatial situation. Ragghianti perceptively observes 'The steep oblique and vertical elevation, completely dominating the field of vision meant that at different heights, and taking into account the vast, mobile landscape of streets and buildings, views had to be established according to constantly changing parameters, new co-ordinates, angles and projections, thereby resulting in many different relationships which became simultaneous, or almost, in the comprehensive act of seeing. The prospects thus acquired a character of potentiality, of possibility, of indefinite and unforeseeable changeability'. C. L. Ragghianti, *Mondrian e l'arte del XX secolo,* Milan, Comunità, 1962.
31 Adopting Ragghianti's interesting thesis (op. cit.) confuting the prejudice, typical of certain critics, that painting anticipates and stimulates a new architecture, one might regard what happened as a mutual exchange. The pictorial 'isms' (Cubism and Futurism) gave back to architecture an extreme elaboration of the same spatial problems which had been mooted in Europe with architecture (the steel architecture of Eiffel and Labrouste and the architecture of Perret, Garnier, Behrens, etc.) in the first decade of the century.

groupings of the Dom-Ino houses were obviously encumbered by unsuccessful attempts to master currently accepted models and still showed obvious allusions to the building projects of Garnier's *cité industrielle*. The arrangement of blocks of elements results in the over-simplified repetition of the module-house, and, although staggered, the pattern is quite symmetrical and does not achieve true integration of the separate building units.

The project for the Pont Butin (1915) for Geneva is unmistakably of classical derivation.

In the *Villa au bord de la Mer* (sea-side house), 1916, one can see distinctly the unresolved conflict between two component styles, one traditional and Mediterranean, revealed in the arches and balcony, the other of a more dynamic character expressed by individual plastic elements (as in the shape of the spiral staircase) and by a freer use of volume ('double' volume) which indicates a step towards a breakaway style.

It was only after he settled finally in Paris (1917) and became a close friend of Amédé Ozenfant that Le Corbusier had any real or rewarding contact with the environment of the cultural *avant-garde* and Cubist painting. His pictorial experiments, initiated under the guidance of Ozenfant, date from this period (November, 1918); they could be described as the first phase of a polemical infiltration of Cubist themes.

Returning to the rationalist tradition of Ledoux ('The circle and the square, these are the letters of the alphabet that authors employ in the design of their best works'; 'The shape of a cube is the symbol of immutability'[32] and of Cézanne ('treat nature by the cylinder, the sphere, the cone . . .'[33] he formulated his Purist maxims: 'Architecture is the scientific, accurate and magnificent play of masses brought together in light. Our eyes are made to see forms in light; light and shade reveal these forms; cubes, cones, spheres, cylinders or pyramids are the great primary forms which light reveals to advantage.'[34]

Perhaps this praise of pure forms reveals an attempt to rely on geometry as some Utopian means of rearranging and reorganising a whole structure which has been thrown dramatically into a state of crisis by the tyranny of war. It is certainly indicative that the first number of the review *L'Esprit Nouveau* (1920) opens with the words 'A great epoch has opened which is animated by a new spirit, a purposeful spirit of construction and synthesis.'

In Purism Le Corbusier identified the potential filter through which the Cubist experience, suitably adapted could penetrate his architectural vocabulary. He foresaw possible scope for advance experimentation in painting from where certain formal themes could later be translated into architecture.[35] These formal themes, Parronchi has noted, were 'on the figurative level, the essence of that world of mechanical structures to which the framework of contemporary life is being reduced'.[36] Then when the full plastic impetus completely invaded the architectural work the experimental function was transferred to sculpture so that Le Corbusier 'connects and integrates pictorial, sculptural and architectonic expression in the same formal concept'.[37] Writing characteristically in the third person, Le Corbusier himself said in 1952, 'in the period called "Purist" he painted only the most banal objects: glasses and bottles, and did not hesitate to avail himself of these simple means to attempt to achieve a plastic solution. It did not matter to him at the time that his paintings were playing a part in the search for new architectural forms. In 1925, however, this goal was achieved. Between

32 Claude-Nicolas Ledoux, *L'Architecture considerée sous le rapport de l'art, des mœurs et de la legislation,* Paris, 1804.
33 From the letter to Emile Bernard, dated April 1904, published in *Paul Cézanne, Letters,* edited by John Rewald, published by Bruno Cassirer, Oxford, 1946 (translated by Marguerite Kay).
34 Le Corbusier, *Vers une Architecture,* Paris, 1923 (*Towards a New Architecture,* introduction by Frederick Etchells, Payson and Clarke Ltd., New York, 1927).
35 While acknowledging the superiority of the vocation of architecture compared to that of painting, one must recognise in the latter the importance of autonomous expression.
36 Alessandro Parronchi, *La Mano aperta di Le Corbusier* in *La Nazione,* Florence, 3rd June, 1963.
37 C. L. Ragghianti, *Le Corbusier à Firenze,* introduction to the catalogue of the exhibition in the Palazzo Strozzi, Florence, 1963.

architectural forms born of reinforced concrete and those of his paintings there was now complete agreement. His painting, like his architecture and even his town-planning, is inspired by the spirit of forms. Without a feeling for or indeed a complete absorption in plasticity and how to arrive at it Le Corbusier would never have created the forms which appeared in the course of his architectural work. The subjects of his pictures went on from the first "glass and bottle" designs to objects which inspired poetical feelings such as roots, pebbles, butchers' bones, the bark of trees, culminating in the human figure, which offers the poetic imagination and the constructive spirit an infinite subject for segmentation and reconstruction, combining plasticity with lyricism within a limited framework.'[38]

The mass-produced living-cell

Architecture is often influenced indirectly or after some delay by certain cultural upheavals, but by war it is affected immediately and directly by devastating social changes. Demographic expansion in the years immediately following the war, rapid resumption of ever-increasing industrialisation, and the resulting phenomenon of the convergence towards metropolitan areas restated with even greater urgency the economic and social aspects of architecture.

The problem could not possibly have been tackled, much less solved, through the aesthetic escapism of the *avant-garde*, which in some cases (Futurism, Suprematism, Constructivism) had simply come to look like premonitory signs of a near-anarchist activism which later became the cultural stimulus of political totalitarian ideologies, destructive of a freely developing social structure.

The peasant masses had suddenly become labourers and had arrived in the city with the immediate goal of regular wages and a housing system limited to the bare essentials. These new users of architecture needed, to start with, low-priced dwellings with minimum comforts which could only be built on the outskirts of the city where the price of land was reasonable because it was far from all the amenities and social services.

Only at a later stage when contact with other social classes aroused a pride complex did these unexpected consumers define for themselves a form of social goal, to attain the 'model' dignity of the middle classes. Then they demanded that the architecture of their homes should be more presentable, and a way of achieving this was to reproduce the threadbare elements of middle-class folk-lore without bothering to take a new standpoint with positive proposals to meet their real needs.

The typical fate of the less educated classes was to pass unexpectedly from the striving for basic necessities into a period of conformity which reflected their satisfaction at having suddenly achieved their confused desires. This slowed down social evolution and produced a dangerous lowering of the level of 'dignity', which produced the irreversible symptoms of an immediate degradation. At this point the groups of improvised shacks were transformed into established peripheral urban forms, detached from the network of social amenities but marked with an apparent exterior decorum, concealing the conditions of some unspecified, 'poorer quarter'. In this way the illusion that mythical prosperity could be attained by the superficial enjoyment of the achievements of the new engineering diverted attention from any real analysis of living conditions.

Called on to resolve the problem of low-cost housing in the new types of building, the architects, by imposing on themselves a method of research which took into account economic, political and social factors, tried to heal the 'class gap' between the old and new urban patterns. It was they who put forward, in the various aspects of their new architectural proposals, a new, meaningful way of life which was neither imitative nor the result of hybrid compromises. These proposals acquainted the consumer with his needs through their use of the new architectural forms.

38 Le Corbusier, *Œuvre complète*, 1946–52, Volume 5, Zurich, 1953.

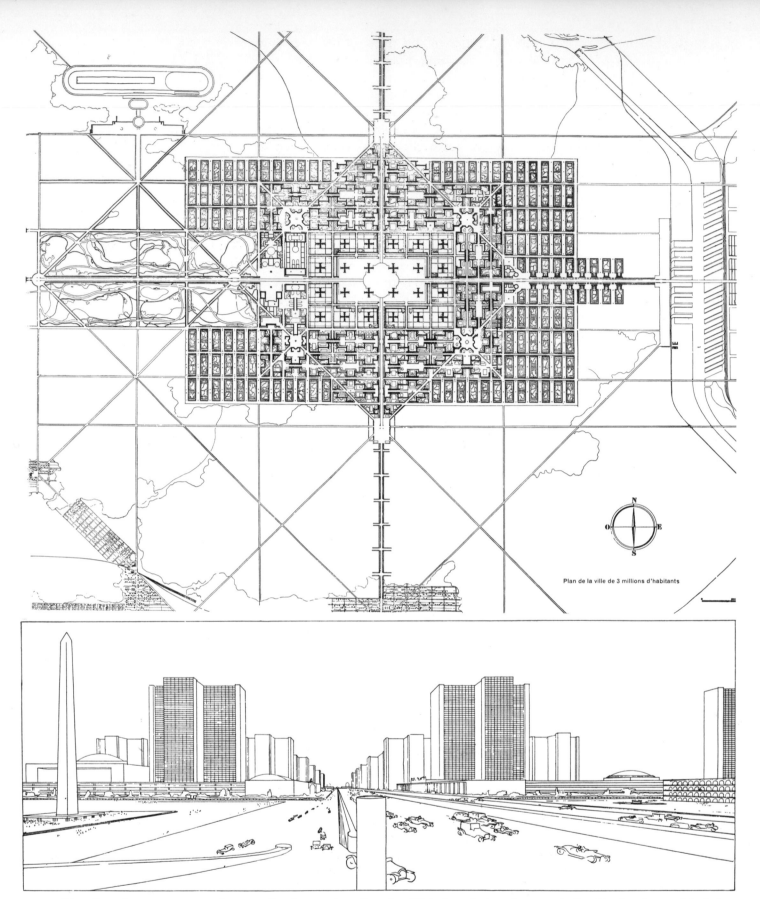

Plan de la ville de 3 millions d'habitants

3 Plan for a 'contemporary city of three million inhabitants'

4 Perspective drawing of 'a contemporary city of three million inhabitants'

In the project for the Citrohan house (1920–2), Le Corbusier tackled the problems of the mass-produced living-cell; 'it is essential to create the right state of mind for mass-produced houses, the state of mind for conceiving mass-produced houses, the state of mind for living in mass-produced houses . . .'[39] However, he did not sacrifice to the demands of mass-production his own conviction of the need to liberate, with 'architecture as a tool', the existential significance which lies at the basis of all human action. 'A standard is established on a firm basis, not capriciously, but with the surety of

39 Le Corbusier, *Vers une Architecture,* op. cit.

18

something intentional and of a logic controlled by analysis and experiment.'[40]

With his free arrangement of internal planes and volumes in the Citrohan house he presented a continuous living-space which made a definitive break with the middle-class concept of living in watertight compartments, in single rooms. It offered a shell in which man could live a much more organised and well-defined life, and provided a substantial and committed answer to day-to-day needs, going far beyond simply the immediate conditions and preparations for occupancy; 'the real needs of a dwelling can be defined and demand a solution. One must take action against the old type of house which made poor use of space. One must . . . think of a house as a machine for living in.'[41] Le Corbusier's house-machine was therefore an instrument that man could use but still govern and adapt to his own specification of life, because it was brought down to the scale which society needed. This was no 'gigantic machine' like that proposed by the Futurists, which 'was to stand on the edge of an abyss in turmoil' to satisfy the needs of individuals 'with the mechanical continuations, accumulators and generators of movement'[42] like some monstrous alienating Moloch ready to devour man cell by cell or to annihilate his personality. Contemporary mechanisation became, therefore, for Le Corbusier *'l'esprit nouveau'* of reality, the mainspring of a new code of ethics which was still this side of the impossible. Many people have turned up their noses at the formula of the *machine à habiter*, but it is nevertheless fascinating as its basic interpretation, summarising in the most economical vocabulary with no accidental unknown quantities, the most true, precise and 'most pertinent'[43] definition of the function of the dwelling in modern civilisation.

Once the living cell and the systematic standardisation of the component parts had been proposed there remained the problem of grouping the cells in relation to the urban environment, the organisation of services and the whole town-planning structure. The need to impose a reasonable appearance, order and proportion to communal spaces and to discover links with surrounding structures within the limits of economic possibilities led Le Corbusier to his first theoretical formulations.

He studied analytically the environmental situations of the old city centres, surrounded and suffocated by the 'scourge of the suburbs' and pin-pointed the problems of inadequate sanitation which symbolised the chronic sclerotisation undermining the centralised network and then put forward a complex structure of proposals suggesting changes to be made at the planning stages. These were expressed in the enunciation of the fundamental principles that the dwelling must be detached from the ground in order to gain room for free access, and that the house must be removed from the 'corridor road' and set in a 'garden-city'.

A construction raised above the ground on *'pilotis'* (columns) allows sun and light to penetrate even beneath the building and, above all, makes possible a radical rethinking concerning the habitation and its environment, a new evaluation of the relationship between the dwelling-place and nature.

As well as adopting the earlier ideas of Perret and Garnier, Le Corbusier raised the concept of the roof-garden to the level of a planned amenity ('Le jardin passe sous la maison, le jardin est aussi sur la maison, sur le toit').[44]

The theory tried out within the living-cell thus formed the foundation for repetition on a wider basis when it came to assembling the various cells. Contrary to his plan for dispersing the urban phenomenon, Le Corbusier, in

40 Le Corbusier, *Vers une Architecture,* op. cit.
41 Le Corbusier, *Œuvre complète,* 1910–29.
42 The quotations are from the Manifesto of Futurist Architecture.
43 The revaluation of the definition '*machine à habiter'* is owed in Italy to Aldo Rossi, 'I do not know of a more pertinent, more exact, and more cultivated definition of the function of the house in modern architecture than that given by . . . This definition is so concise that it still arouses the contempt of many critics, but it is much more than a slogan. It is the most revolutionary definition in modern architecture' (in *Casabella* 246, 1960, page 4).
44 Le Corbusier, *Œuvre complète,* 1910–29.

order to ward off 'isolation and disillusionment in the garden-city', arranged the single cells vertically, concentrating them into large complexes which he called '*immeubles-villas*'.

The plan for the Citrohan house, but with its terrace-garden transferred inside, and proposed as a repeatable element on the straight line of a balcony running high round the building, represented the interpretation on an urban scale of a concept and organisation of life inspired by a Certosa monastery in Italy.[45] 'The *immeubles-villas* propose a new formula for urban dwelling. Each apartment is really a small house with a garden, located at any height. But the street itself is modified, it stands away from the buildings and trees invade the city; the density of the residential quarters remains the same as today but the buildings are higher, opening enlarged perspectives.'[46]

The weak point in the development of Le Corbusier's theories is that he should have attempted to tackle the complex phenomenon which beset an urban organism by a method based on the repetition of schemes tested only in such a limited context as the living-cell. Giorgio Piccinato justly observes that the view 'from inside conditions all the theoretical elaboration of the modern movement, until in the vastness of the buildings realised in the post-war period, one is not far from considering the complexity of the urban phenomenon as the sum of tested minor phenomena. It is essential to realise, however, that in the present climate of critical review, the given idealistic solution which distinguishes the work of Le Corbusier takes on a new attractiveness; this is coming about because the dimensions of living are so altered that the new problems can only be solved by proposals for radical changes, however idealistic or impracticable they might seem. It is, in fact, true that Le Corbusier builds up his towns through research into the types of dwellings and his solution, even if idealistic, is very precise and complete compared to that of Gropius, Taut or Mies van der Rohe . . .'[47]

A contemporary city of three million inhabitants

Figs. 3, 4.

Le Corbusier's plan for a 'contemporary city of three million inhabitants'[48] deliberately avoids the limitations resulting from the decentralisation and enlargement of cities. Instead, here is a theoretical attempt to outline a new city-structure, organised with the guiding principle of decongesting the central nucleus by means of fast-flowing traffic routes across its whole linear development and planning for the density of population increase to be parallel to the spread of green and tree-planted areas. Even if the plan is drawn up along academic lines,[49] the new structure is developed on a scale which has as its constant unit of reference that it is the primary machine of man. The network of roads is set out as a basic element of reference by means of which are tackled and resolved all the different questions of ratio concerning the presence and size of the pedestrian, the car, and at the extreme, the aeroplane.

As an answer to the possibility of a life measured by the yardstick of contemporary dynamism, which was invading the urban context and was most characteristically reflected in the new concept of living in the city, Le Corbusier's relevant, if theoretical reply represented a victory over the 'isms' of the *avant-garde* which were swiftly and decisively stopped in their tracks

45 On this topic Le Corbusier says: 'As far as I am concerned these studies have their origin in a visit in 1907 to the Certosa d'Ema near Florence. In that musical, Tuscan countryside I saw a "modern city" crowning the hilltop. Its profile was the most noble of the surrounding landscape, the uninterrupted crown of monks' cells, each opening on to a garden enclosed on the inside. I do not think I shall ever again encounter another such joyous interpretation of a dwelling. The back of each cell opened on to a way covered by a portico, which was the cloister used for communal purposes: prayer, visiting, meals, funerals. This "modern city" dates from the fifteenth century. The radiant vision of it will remain with me for ever.' (Quoted by F. Tentori, *Le Corbusier*, Milan, 1965.) The same model was consulted again on the occasion of the project of the convent of La Tourette.
46 Le Corbusier, *Œuvre complète*, 1910–29.
47 Giorgio Piccinato, op. cit. Chapter III, *Metodologia di Le Corbusier*.
48 The plan was shown for the first time in Paris in November, 1922, at the *Salon d'Automme*.
49 Despite its strict orthogonal projection, the plan for the city of three million inhabitants is still from a formal aspect; subject to imitation today, proof enough lies in the most recent proposal for the administrative centre of Florence (1967) which is the result of a questionable assembling of different elements 'already prearranged and in themselves aesthetically determined' (drawn from projects destined for the cities of Turin, Kyoto, Berlin, and Runcorn New Town), mounted in a setting closely reminiscent of the old design of Le Corbusier's plan (see *Firenze uno e due, La Nuova Italia*, Florence, 1967).

in admiration. The pompous and artificial amenities of Sant'Elia's Futurist city are completely detached from reality and his metaphysical notions unbacked by any logical structural organisation.[50]

Le Corbusier's project for a 'contemporary city' is not accompanied by any manifesto but by an extremely informative technical report in which he explained in detail the principles behind the organisation of his ideal urban structure. Furthermore one can detect in his report an assessment, an awareness of the practical things that would have to be shouldered by the people living there.

A logical hierarchy determines the different levels of trunk roads intersecting beneath a wide, reinforced concrete landing-platform for air taxis and the highways for fast traffic which cut diagonally across the urban network. A cogent method of distribution governs the lay-out of the administrative centre, the public buildings, the town hall and the museum, side by side with the administrative block, characterised by skyscrapers sixty floors high and of cruciform plan for offices and hotels, with services, shops, cinemas and theatres at the lower levels. Green parks are laid out with residential installations of the 'open' type, dwellings of six floors à redents, and of the 'closed' type surrounding a large internal rectangular space of about 90 × 300 metres. The outside of this type of dwelling has already been described when discussing the dwelling typical of the immeuble-villa.

The whole of Le Corbusier's project reflects the lucid thinking of a strict ideology and takes into account all the economic, political, scientific and social circumstances affecting the definition of an urban installation, both internally and in relation to the outside world.

For Le Corbusier these considerations were constants on both theoretical and practical levels in his diagrammatic graph of the phenomenon of the structural organisation of a city and he did not miss an opportunity to demonstrate that they were applicable, even when brought down to the scale of everyday living. He took advantage of his work on the *Pavillon de l'Esprit Nouveau*, at the International Exhibition of the Decorative Arts in Paris (1925) as an opportunity of constructing a model version of one living-cell unit of the *immeuble-villa*. This was a testing of his proposal for a new order of life for the individual within the compass of a collective system, which he solved with a measure of non-conformity and an unusual freedom of space. In the prototype one can see the various influences which have infiltrated and been absorbed into his experience. One can gauge the importance of his organised lay-out which was in fact a point of departure for a complex creative process, passing through various purifying stages and new conceptions of space to find a definitive version in the living-cell for his *Unité d'habitation* at Marseilles. This in turn was part of the patient research and controversial tension directed towards the primary target of the *ville radieuse*. As functional problems were solved, so the form developed and gained character.

The free scheme of the façade of the Villa at Vaucresson (1922) which is the logical external effect of the arrangement of interior planes and volumes, is perfected and strictly applied in the *'tracés régulateurs'*. These *'tracés régulateurs'* were essential to the development of the formal themes of the Maison de la Roche (1923) of the housing at Pessac (1925).

Methodical perseverance, continual research and consistent principles give the impression, in Le Corbusier's statements over the years, of piling up

Five points for a new architecture

50 If Sant'Elia's work is regarded again in the light of an independent study, free from all mythical super-structures and defined within its valid limits, it will be seen as an expression of the new Italian architectonic cultural context of its time, as the expression of a state of mental inertia. It represents the private unfinished elaboration of an inspiration (outraged and betrayed by the publicity platform of the Futurists) which was faithfully followed as far as vision allowed. But it was never quite reached or conquered because insufficient experience and lack of technical knowledge did not stand up to the real everyday demands. Nevertheless Sant'Elia's 'new city' does have a contribution to make, if only as an additional stimulus to the awareness of problems that modern dynamism promotes in determining a new space for the urban complex.

repetitively like so many sterile variations but when a new problem arises and they are restated, they have new and increased validity. In fact, his arguments undergo an uninterrupted process of revision, finally leading to what is absolutely essential, revealing all the fascination of reform and making its inner significance understandable.

In the same way Le Corbusier's elaboration of the 'five points' for a new architecture[51] is discernible in previous statements which he now systematised. In the *plan Voisin* the formula of the 'contemporary city' is transferred from an imaginary site to the *rive droite* in Paris. In its successive phases (1922, 1925, 1930, 1937, 1946), this plan characteristically represents a study perfected over the years, constantly added to with new ideas, new forms and continually checked against the unfailing measure of the principles he had adopted.

The five points are the outcome. They 'open new perspectives to architecture and these are extended to town-planning which can find in them the means to bring a solution to the great sickness of today's cities'.[52] They are the codification of all the triumphs of European architecture between the two wars, including external influences, and they represent not only the means of liberation from the eighteenth-century tradition, but also a breaking away from the traditions which fettered all subsequent architecture.

On columns

The house on columns! The house used to be sunk into the ground, with dark and often humid rooms. Reinforced concrete brought the notion of using *pilotis* or columns. The house is thereby raised above the ground, the garden passing underneath the house. There is also a garden on top of the house, on the roof.

Roof-gardens

For centuries a traditional pitched roof supported the winter layer of snow, while the house was heated by stoves. From the moment that central heating was installed, the traditional roof ceased to be convenient. The roof should no longer be convex but concave, making rain-water flow towards the interior, not the exterior of the house. This is a universal truth: cold climates should eliminate the sloping roofs, requiring instead the construction of concave roof-terraces with water draining towards the interior of the house. Reinforced concrete is the new means for realising a homogeneous roofing but is subject to a great deal of expansion and contraction. An intense movement of this sort can cause cracks in the structure. Instead of trying to drain away all the rain-water, one should maintain a constant humidity for the concrete of the roof-terrace and thereby assure a regulated temperature for the concrete. An especially good protection: sand covered by thick cement slabs laid loosely together, the cracks being seeded with grass. The sand and roots permit the slow infiltration of the rain-water. The garden-terraces become luxuriant: flowers, shrubbery and trees, lawns. Thus we are led to choose the roof-terrace for technical reasons, economic reasons, reasons of comfort and sentimental reasons.

Open plan

Until now load-bearing walls rising up from the basement, were always superimposed, forming the ground and upper floors, right up to the roof. The structural plan was utterly dependent on these load-bearing walls. The introduction of reinforced concrete into the house results in a free and open plan. The floors no longer need to have superimposed rooms of the same size. Everything is optional. There is a consequent economy of constructed volume, a rigorous use of each centimetre, resulting in turn in great financial economy. The new plan is therefore easily rationalised.

51 Published in the *Œuvre complète*, 1910–29, in collaboration with Pierre Jeanneret.
52 Le Corbusier, op. cit.

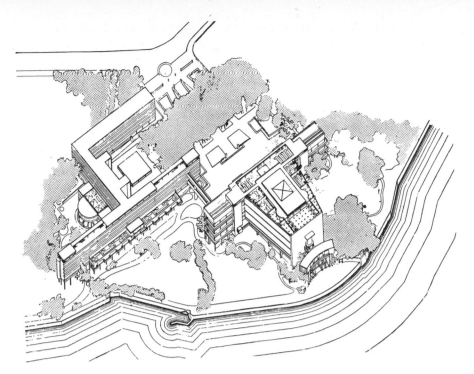

Walls of Glass

The window is one of the essential features of the house. Progress has also liberated the window. Reinforced concrete has brought about a revolution in the history of the window. Windows can now run from one edge of the façade to the other. The window is a repeatable, serviceable element of the house, for all town-houses, workers' houses, and apartment houses.

Free façades

The columns are now set back from the façades towards the interior of the house. The exterior walls are no longer load-bearing and can be opened up or closed, with windows or insulating elements at will to satisfy aesthetic or functional requirements.[53]

In the 'five points' therefore, one finds, supported by briefly outlined but effective arguments, all the distinguishing characteristics of the new architectonic figuration, which, when rationalised according to the golden grid of the *'tracé régulateur'*, take on the familiar appearance of vehicles of form which occur in all Le Corbusier's work, with pertinent variations in certain cases.

In the Villa Stein at Garches (1927) the basic scheme of horizontal elements outlining the composition of the façades as if it were a transparent box, alternates inside, on the first floor and the roof-garden with complete freedom of planes, which emerge rhythmically in relief. These are reflected on the exterior where they might seem to be an irrational addition or interference, conflicting with the rigidly strict *'tracé régulateur'*.

These emergent shapes, which are superimposed in dialectic relation without disturbing the pre-ordained logic of their support, are the forerunners of a potential plastic energy, temporarily restrained by a form of Cartesian logic, but later freely unleashed in the unique spatial experience of Ronchamp.

The project for the competition for the Palace of the League of Nations at Geneva was a recapitulation of previous experiences for Le Corbusier. The theme had a fascinating attraction for an architect who had faith in mankind and believed that the community spirit could improve relations between men. Le Corbusier submitted a design for a *maison de travail* ('a place to work in'), corresponding to contemporary requirements, an architecture informed

The Villa Stein at Garches

Pls. 1, 2, 3

Political issues

Fig. 5

53 Le Corbusier, op. cit.

with a 'new aesthetic conforming to the general evolution of society'.[54]

He was perhaps the only one among 377 competitors to understand that on this occasion the architecture had to interpret an ideal and emphasise the embodiment of hope in this new international structure. He understood that a League of Nations had to be not only a complex representative organism, but a working body, in order to achieve an effective spirit of co-operation and to assure the peace sought by peoples everywhere.

'But the governors did not seem to work along the same lines as the masses they governed and diplomats have an annoying propensity for the gilded halls of dead kings.'[55]

If he had only submitted 'the stately theme to his usual functional analysis',[56] the project would certainly not have reached its 'breaking-point', that level of commitment which became a definite new cultural proposition.

Le Corbusier wanted above all to clear the subject of all its rhetorical appendages, reveal all its mysteries and express the potential significance of a free and neutral association between nations.

These factors were more important in inspiring his work than any facile analysis of the functional requirements of the organism. In fact, the functional aspects were regarded quite kindly by the jury and were later imitated. It was his extremely non-conformist message to which objection was made and which threw the already disintegrating organisation (which the jury officially represented) into a state of complete panic. The project submitted jointly by Le Corbusier and Pierre Jeanneret was fated not to be the winner. After sixty-five sittings the jury, which had purposely ignored all the superficial pomp which such occasions usually demanded, discovered with puritanical strictness, that the plan was not drawn in Indian ink as stipulated in the competition rules. Later, behind a monumental smokescreen of false architecture, the League of Nations, a mausoleum of illusions, was to be revealed as a bankrupt organisation paralysed by diplomatic compromises, incapable of anticipating Nazi and Fascist aggression and preoccupied with hiding, behind hypocritical condemnation and sterile sanctions, its own inconsistency and inability to safeguard the people's rights and the peace of the world.

On the human level, the Geneva competition with the jury's lack of understanding and his exclusion from deserved recognition was a bitter pill for Le Corbusier. But he emerged from the shattering experience better disposed towards controversy, more resolute before criticism, prepared to do battle with official conformity and the lingering obstruction of the Academies and determined to demonstrate the truth of what he foresaw for the future.

It was not Le Corbusier who was the great loser at Geneva, but the 'new spirit' which was simply not understood by an inquiring society. Its full import, as a breaking-away with completely new proposals, was not grasped. Perhaps this was understandable in a Europe governed by confused ideals, buffeted between the democratic system and the new national flattery of dictatorships, but surely it could not be so in Russia, a country where revolution had violently overthrown all old structures in order to build a new one, one where Le Corbusier's work was already accepted and appreciated.[57]

Fig. 6
Nevertheless, the competition for the Palace of the Soviets (1931) demonstrated that even if the basic conditions and ideological promises had been shaken the result was still the same. The moral and cultural adventure of modern architecture ended in bankruptcy in Moscow as in Geneva. Anyone who believed, like Le Corbusier, that the new architecture, with its anti-traditional and anti-rhetorical language, its fundamentality and careful con-

---

54 Le Corbusier, *Œuvre complète*, 1910–29.
55 Le Corbusier, *Œuvre complète*, 1910–29.
56 L. Benvolo, op. cit., Vol. II, Chapter XIV.
57 In 1929 Le Corbusier designed for Moscow the building of the Central Offices of the Co-operative Unions of the U.S.S.R. (The Centrosoyus.) The building was intended to be an opportunity for the application of all new technical advances and thus a prototype of architecture drawn from modern scientific achievements.

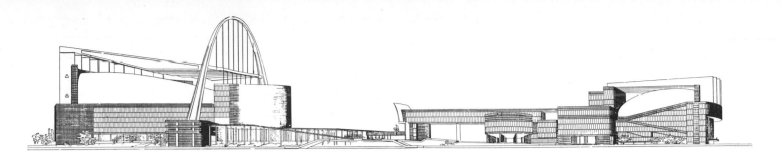

sideration of human needs, could fittingly interpret the young Soviet social reality, was to be disappointed.

The project that Le Corbusier submitted stemmed from the basic principle that each man is more than ever on the same level as other men, in the process of realising a 'horizontal' type of society. The unusual articulation of the long complex along an axis blocked at both ends by the facing masses of two auditoriums eliminated any possible hierarchical stratification or pompous distractions. The building is a complex machine (one's immediate reaction is that it looks like a factory) made explicit by its materials (steel and concrete), its only moments of formal escapism being the acrobatic structures of the two auditoriums.

In the meantime, however, the Party machine had become an even more bureaucratic structure of pyramidal type, with an absolute dictator at the summit who would neither admit nor tolerate any horizontal levelling and who, with the *avant-garde* out of the way, set about decreeing what sort of art should reflect social realism.

Even Gropius's project, whose radial plan (dependent sectors radiating from the centre) was also an open denunciation of the symbolism of hierarchy, was pronounced to be too flat. Once again, therefore, knowing perfectly well what art flatters vanity, the decrepit academy triumphed over the modern architecture which was considered non-Marxist, so that this time its victory was in the name not of conservatism but of socialism. Thus it was that the Russian Jofan, canny interpreter of the way the Soviet system was progressing, produced a vulgar layer cake, crammed with columns and balusters and topped with the inevitable, pompous, commemorative statues, a concrete symbol of the power and megalomania of the régime.

Pls. 4 to 7, Fig. 7   In the period between these two competitions, Le Corbusier designed and built the Villa Savoye at Poissy (1929–31) and the Swiss pavilion in the *cité universitaire* in Paris (1930–2). These two works mark the resumption of experiments with certain problems and ideas on the level of a micro-society, with the not surprising ambition of eventually translating them into a larger scale and testing them on the level of systems which govern the world: 'those buildings played the role of laboratories. We wanted every element built during those years to be tried and tested proof which would allow us, with complete confidence, to take the necessary initiative in the field of town-planning.'[58] As a matter of policy it was still risky to pass from a limited to a wider scale, but it was acceptable in these cases and was an incentive for the realisation of two masterpieces.

The Villa Savoye seems to grow from the interior, almost as though reacting against any form of external 'front', thanks to a central force, which is almost forcefully expressed in the continuity of the spiral staircase, but which loses its intensity towards the outside walls, which balance the external environment with the internal forces. The staircase, an 'architectural promenade' which leads to the 'lyrical experience of the purely plastic',[59] achieves vertically an accelerated communication between consecutive spatial experiences: the first moment of contact at ground level, the moment of interim passage and arrival at the middle zone and final freedom from tension at roof-garden level. Three moments, three different stages of life, where all the basic symbols of architecture are organised in synthesis and finally meet in culmination.

Pl. 8, Fig. 8   In the Swiss pavilion, the elements of a vocabulary of form are even more evident, superimposed on a framework of Cartesian logic. The curving wall of the tower which houses the stairs and services reinforces with its physical continuity the basic theme of the north wall; it is an emphatic symbol of a desire to shelter, in striking contrast with the transparency of the glazed screen of the south wall. When one reaches the point of moulding the material of architecture and disposing its constitutional elements with Le

58 Le Corbusier, introduction to the *Œuvre complète*, 1929–34.
59 B. Zevi, op. cit., Chapter III.

9–10 Sketch for the town-planning scheme for Rio de Janeiro

11 Sketch for the town-planning scheme for Montevideo

12 Sketch for the town-planning scheme of São Paulo, Brazil

13 'Plan obus' for the restructuring of Algiers

Corbusier's nonchalant authority, it means that the formative stage has been over for some time. It means that the potential models, consulted initially, have undergone critical appraisal, their value has been assessed and the degree of truth and inspiration they contain fathomed until something new is achieved. A phase of the 'compositional domination' is thus reached by a logical sequence and expressed in an inexhaustibly inventive vocabulary which becomes a new source of reference. In Le Corbusier's passionately active commitment one can distinguish, according to one's subjective preference, when 'theorem prevails over inspiration'[60] and when inspiration, bursting through in powerful statements of form, prevails over theorem. When one is entirely objective, it is always clear how, never weakened by any doubt of the ideal, the determined, steadfast search continues unremittingly for a suitable method of creating, through architecture and town-planning, a fitting environment for a more progressive and happier society.

The great town-planning schemes

After the 'architectural revolution', town-planning became the 'major preoccupation'.

Le Corbusier's town-planning projects are architectural operations on an urban scale. They originate in a feeling for form inspired by the complex integral mass of the site and find content and order in pattern of substructures.

For Le Corbusier a city's development is already implicit in nature and in the city's history. It is a question of knowing how to read the different layers, examine the surrounding environment, capture the form of the landscape and recognise the characteristics imposed by the climate.

He said that 'it is through town-planning and architecture that environment and landscape can become part of the city and even a decisive figurative and spiritual factor in it.'[61] Architecture must therefore itself become constructed landscape, a constituent element of a landscape of human geography.

If nature is to become a vehicle for creative exploitation, architecture must be so adapted as to avail itself of natural elements. In bringing formal man-made elements into line with those of the geographical environment, it was obviously Le Corbusier's intention to achieve a biological unity which comes close to the Cartesian concept of universal order and of unity between works of nature and works of human intelligence: 'the unity which is in nature and in man is the law which endows his works with life'.[62] In other words, it means putting the man-made elements in dialectic contact with nature, or else giving nature, an external agent, a supporting role to an artificial presence.

His notes of 1929 for the town-planning schemes for Rio de Janeiro,

60 B. Zevi, op. cit., Chapter III.
61 Le Corbusier, *Manière de Penser l'Urbanisme*. Chapter VI: *Acquisition d'un outillage*. 'Par l'urbanisme et par l'architecture les sites et le paysage peuvent entrer dans la ville, ou de la ville constituer un élément plastique et sensible décisif.'
62 Le Corbusier, op. cit., Chapter V: *Les Règles: Humain et Nature*. 'L'unité qui est dans la nature et dans l'homme, c'est cette loi qui prête vie aux ouvrages.'

Montevideo and São Paulo of Brazil are full of this spirit. After a swift look Figs. 9–12 at the conditions of the natural surroundings, Le Corbusier, with a clear-thinking decisiveness which seems almost like improvisation or over-simplification, made sweeping suggestions of a kind that would completely transform the way of life and living conditions in the city.

Enormous viaducts, along which run motorways, wind round the undu-lating natural curve of Rio and, all the way, dominate views of either side of the bay and of mountains. At Montevideo they extend into the sea in search of wider vistas. At another point they intersect on different levels, as in the primary network of the linear development of São Paulo, where they stretch to the four horizons following a more uniform landscape. They appear at first sight to be acts of violence against nature; on closer examina-tion, one can see that they are closely integrated with it, corresponding in form and size.

The foundation for such audacious ideas was based on an analysis of the arrangement of ancient cities, particularly the towns of Roman Gaul, which resulted in the principle of 'deliberated form', that is, a type of design which integrates unknown factors, but makes full use of town-planning elements to be certain of achieving favourable living conditions.[63]

The idea of establishing a prearranged form might be considered a type of active mediation between an 'urban pattern' and the 'natural features of the land' so that the artificial elements created by man follow on from the natural conditions.

Following these early experiments and in line with his standard principles, Le Corbusier undertook, in 1930, a town-planning scheme for Algiers. 'The project for Algiers is a town-planning scheme for a city in which are con-centrated the history of two civilisations, a difficult topography with magnifi-cent landscapes, a geographical environment which is part of two continents and a future full of potential on the threshold of a continent embarking on a new course. The plan reveals a sureness of hand due to clear principles, variety and flexibility, the fruit of a happy marriage between man and nature, between everyday reality and lofty ideals.'[64]

The 'plan obus' is an urban pattern based on the idea of having a vertical Fig. 13 garden-city running for miles high up along the cliff-tops and a new business city occupying the shore, housed in two enormous blocks jutting out into the tip of Cap d'Algers, joined by a suspended footbridge to the new residen-tial city. The latter is developed in 'tensional networks that are curved and linked together'[65] along the hilly slopes of Fort l'Empéreur. A highway 100 metres above sea-level links the outer suburbs; beneath the level for vehicles is one for garages, while the rest of the viaduct is formed of superimposed floors with an average height of 4·5 metres, between floors which are in fact the various levels of a garden-city.

The 180,000 inhabitants of this viaduct city are assured of 'a splendid view of the sea and cliffs, immediate accessibility to the upper motorway (100 metres above sea-level) and with the lower motorway underneath the *pilotis*.[66] Dwellings are inserted into the long cement honeycomb, there is even room for Arab-style buildings with horseshoe arches and little balconies on brackets. Artificial floors at various levels allow for further additions. Even if the compelling logic of figures and arguments which illustrate the economic advantages of this type of urbanisation may be viewed today with sceptical complacency, one ought to take another look at the inventiveness of the organisational and of the figurative aspect of these architectural town-

63 These ideas are expressed in Chapter VI of the op. cit. *Acquisition d'un outillage.*
64 Le Corbusier, op. cit., Chapter IX. '*Il ne s'agit pas d'idées toutes faites*'. 'Le croquis d'Alger exprimant l'urbanisation d'une ville ou se conjuguent l'histoire de deux civilisations, une topographie difficile offrant les plus beaux paysages, une géographie étendue à deux continents, un avenir prodigieux, révèle la fermeté due aux principes clairs, la diversité et la souplesse, produits d'un mariage heureux entre hommes et nature, entre réalité quotidienne et intention élevée.'
65 C. L. Ragghianti, *Le Corbusier à Firenze*, introduction to the catalogue of the exhibition at the Palazzo Strozzi, Florence, 1963.
66 Le Corbusier, *Œuvre complète, 1929–34.*

planning proposals. They establish a hitherto unknown co-existence of relationships and a whole scale of operations which are today considered essential when tackling the problems of planning a metropolis in proportion to the over-enlargement of its administrative centres.

The invention of a new form of city has always been a major objective for those in power in every era, an aspiration whose achievement would provide permanent evidence of the culture of the time. The pre-planned form of Roman towns and the subsequent spontaneous outcrops of the Middle Ages, clustered round political and religious centres, were followed in the Renaissance by an explicit demand for a new city design. In plans drawn up for 'ideal cities' Filarete or Francesco di Giorgio aimed to show the need for an urban pattern which would represent the new concept of space resulting from the science of perspective and the new social and political order. For the first time a city was planned from scratch, envisaged as an extended complex building, worked out in every detail, in other words adopting criteria which turned out to be quite like present-day methods of town-planning.

After this Renaissance attempt, which never got further than the theoretical stage, subsequent cultures did not invent new city-structures. 'Baroque' society brought additions and variations to individual buildings within the old shape of the medieval city but this had only a partial effect on the structure of the urban network. Not even social upheavals following the French Revolution provided what was necessary for the invention of a new city. Neo-Classicism, which at least gave formal confirmation of ethical values by using the elements and experience of classical tradition, translated the new excitements into spatial terms but did not produce a different city design. The socialist ideologies of Owen and Fourier finally envisaged town-planning installations which were no more than different forms of emphatic reiterations of classical lay-outs. Garnier's 'industrial city' and Howard's 'garden-city' broached important sectoral problems and perfected certain proposals but complete liberation of the city from the point of view of a total innovation in both plan and form was never achieved in nineteenth-century schemes.

It is only with Le Corbusier that a strong, inventive urban design finally emerged, which was attuned to the problems of its own time and then not the Le Corbusier of the 'contemporary city', hampered by academic restrictions, but the architect of the plans for Rio and Algiers.

The viaduct-cities, superimposed with powerful effect over the traditional city outlines were the most outstanding features of the new formula. They represented a channelling of new energy generated from the spirit of contemporary mechanisation and clearly celebrated the concept of organising cities vertically in relation to specific geographical conditions. They represented the outward forms of a continuous integration between town and country, involving the breaking down of all old social barriers and class distinctions. Finally they represented a new and definite direction for the destiny of the city. But this promise of a new city was a vision far too advanced and radical for the times, or at least it required a much higher level of understanding of urban phenomena than had been reached up to then. Only in more recent years has it been possible to trace the guiding motifs of Le Corbusier's town-planning predictions of the thirties in certain interesting projects of contemporary Japanese architecture.

Kenzo Tange's plans for Boston (1959) and Tokyo (1960) show, in the arrangement of services, streets and dwellings on different levels, incorporated in long load-bearing structures, echoes of Le Corbusier's earlier themes, but developed to suit contemporary requirements and backed by more thorough and appropriate technological investigation. 'An organisation of this type,' writes Tange, in the report of the Boston project, 'is an expression of the hierarchy of the various levels: nature, intercommunication, collectivity tied to social functions, and finally the human scale of individual life. At the local level the details and organisation of the house itself can be arranged

at will according to taste.'[67] Rediscovered and restated after thirty years in almost identical language, Le Corbusier's idea seems even more up-to-date, practical, inventive and full of potential.

La ville radieuse (the radial city)

Le Corbusier's town-planning projects in their time seemed to be so much impracticable prophetising, but the strict policy behind them, typical of this phase of his work and thought, explains his critical attitude towards Manhattan's skyscrapers which were then the most tangible expression of architectural achievement. 'The skyscrapers of New York are romantic; a gesture of pride, and that has importance of course . . . But the street has been killed and the city made into a mad-house.'[68] 'Here the skyscraper is not an element in city-planning, but a banner in the sky, a fireworks rocket, an aigrette in the coiffure of a name henceforth listed in the financial Almanach de Gotha.'[69]

His reaction was to put forward other proposals for Manhattan, in place of the romantic skyscraper he produced the 'Cartesian skyscraper' (1935). The Cartesian skyscraper was destined to be the prototype of the administrative buildings later included in the more extensive network of the *ville radieuse*. In time it underwent different planimetric variations until it was transformed into a vertical skyscraper.

Fig. 14

It was out of a combination and elaboration of two types of buildings (the Cartesian skyscraper and the '*immeuble-villa*') that the new organism of the *unité d'habitation* was born. It is in fact a portion, or a partial version of the viaduct-city and for that reason more within the realms of possibility.

67 Quoted in *Casabella*, No. 258, 1961.
68 Le Corbusier, *When the Cathedrals were white. A journey to the country of timid people*. Translated by Francis E. Hyslop, Jr, New York, 1947.
69 Le Corbusier, op. cit.

Here the idea of a highway on the roof was abandoned, for obvious reasons, and gave way to an interior street on a suitable scale. Instead, the roof-garden returned to the top of the building while the shell of the building was suspended on stilts over ground left free for amenities.

Throughout Le Corbusier's career he shows a constant capacity to produce a range of valid, logical variations and amplifications of a few basic themes, which, with repetition, assume the character of 'animated convictions'.[70] During the forced isolation of the war years, Le Corbusier sought refuge in his ivory tower of thought and reflection. From 1939 to 1945, he collected together and put in order, in *La Charte d'Athènes* and *Les Trois Etablissements Humains*, all the developments and perfections that over the years had improved his scant but vital town-planning statements. The preface of *La Charte d'Athènes* is an examination of time as a definitive element as in architecture and town-planning: 'the solar day of twenty-four hours dictates the rhythm of man's activity'. It seems an unimportant and practically marginal statement, but in fact it draws attention to a natural, unalterable and wrongly overlooked rule which links man to his dwelling, to his free time, and to his place of work in a perfect sequence.

In his introduction Jean Giraudoux shows precisely the psychological and physical effects that strike man when his sequence of actions is not logically co-ordinated with time: 'a citizen sets out every morning for his work heavily burdened and returns in the evening with unnecessary difficulty, delays and worries. This continual sapping of daily pleasure, and the need to adapt to conditions of unrelieved mediocrity and the compromises this imposes on heart and body rob man's spirit of the qualities and inquisitiveness proper to it.' Giraudoux also understands the higher political significance of Le Corbusier's involvement which outlines remedies for what *La Charte d'Athènes* calls the reasons for the 'inhumanity of cities'.

The 'doctrinal points', laying down courses of action, aim to establish that 'the city should ensure individual freedom on spiritual and material levels and the advantages of collective living'.

To achieve this goal, to satisfy this seemingly contradictory principle, the 'size of everything within the urban mechanism can only be regulated on a human scale. Man's natural measurements must serve as a basis for all the standards relating to life and to the different functions of existence'.[71] Faced with the reality of the usual conditions of living, working and recreation in today's cities, the most fitting corrective action can be summed up in the four fundamental town-planning functions: (1) To ensure healthy housing. (2) To organise places of work. (3) To provide the necessary amenities for beneficial use of free time. (4) To establish connections between these different organisations with a traffic network which guarantees circulation but respects the prerogatives of each of the former.

This means that creativity must be brought into the process of transformation in order to overcome the heavy obstacle of habit, and this creativity take account of the different activities and aims which distinguish regional environments from the wider national context.

The main aims of town-planning as set out in *La Charte d'Athènes* are stated again in essence in *Les Trois Etablissements Humains*. But here they are proposed on the larger scale of a more extensive area, in the higher interest of 'qualifying' material conditions. 'Qualification is a virtue deep-rooted in man's being which can usually be called forth. Standpoint, which puts man above events, allowing him to act better. Spirit, which can illuminate all everyday happenings. It is this that removed boredom and enlightens our existence.'[72]

70 C. L. Ragghianti, op. cit.
71 Le Corbusier, *La Charte d'Athènes,* Groupe C.I.A.M. France. With an introduction by Jean Giraudoux, Plon, Paris, 1943.
72 Le Corbusier, *Les Trois établissements humains*. Urbanisme des C.I.A.M. Collection Ascoral (under the direction of Le Corbusier). Part II. *Ethique du travail*. 'La qualification, vertu rattachée au fond même de l'être peut éveiller en beaucoup un dieu qui dort. Prise de position qui situe l'homme au-dessus de l'événement lui permettant de se mieux conduire. Esprit qui peut éclairer tous les actes du quotidien. Voilà qui écarte l'ennui. Voilà qui éclaire l'existence.'

'Qualification' is in the long run the moral rule which the three establishments must obey, because as they are distributed over a given territory and organised into a real 'constructed biology', they answer specific needs. Thus unit agricultural production, which gives a new look to conditions of life and production in the country, is linked to the radial concentric city by intercommunicating routes. The latter, by self-definition, becomes the commercial, intellectual and administrative centre of the government and is in turn connected with the linear industrial city in a logical and harmonious order which proves to be the best tool applicable to a 'working civilisation' anticipated to be moving towards irreversible success. The 'green factory' ('l'usine verte') is the model unit of the linear city and takes the place of the 'black factory' of the first phase of industrialisation. It brings work back into a natural environment. By introducing elements of distraction and relaxation, it gives a new meaning to working hours, transforming from 'suffering into joy this time which takes up the greater part of life'.[73] Dignity and joy of life are the moral factors that the green factory claims to bring to the physical discipline of work.

With the achievement of these objectives comes the discipline demanded by a natural sequence of working operations and thus a co-ordination of human activity in time and space. It becomes possible to transfer the capillary organisation to the whole territory until ideally, circuits of work and production may be thought of as channels of life, like arteries, uniting continental and inter-continental systems in organised, well-balanced structures.

The logical conclusion is thus that the 'linear city' is a 'constituent element – and one of the most essential – of the future constitution of the world . . . a theme by its very nature destined for international discussion round a green baize table'.[74]

In the summer of 1945 when Europe was rising from the smouldering funeral pyre of war and her newly liberated people were preparing to meet round a green baize table to establish some programme and direction for a new life, there loomed in the East the sinister mushroom-shaped shadow of Hiroshima's atomic bomb. Once again a new world epoch began with the foreboding of destruction.

It is when one realises the precariousness of the future that the spiritual need for present security is revealed; and at that particularly delicate moment the present was represented by a desire to rebuild in order to forget. Rebuilding meant entrusting man with all the phenomena of the world, relying on his ability to hope again, on his logical desire to recreate order, and on strict scientific standards. Rebuilding meant, in fact, rebirth; rebirth, as adults and in a new reality, also meant channelling the new demands of an expectant society and without rhetoric or banter satisfying them with the rational results of a unitary and resolute rule founded on the universal measure of man.

The time was therefore ripe for a return to man, to the measurement of man, in order to find a matrix of the right proportion to relate to society and rediscover the unknown quantity which has always solved the equation of the world.

On this occasion too, Le Corbusier lived up to his vocation, perceiving and registering the tensions related to the stresses of the moment; sensitive interpreter of the situation, he agreed that 'in order to work out the answers to the formidable problems presented by our time and with regard to its "equipment", there is only one acceptable criterion which will reduce every

From l'Unité d'habitation to Ronchamp

15 The Modulor

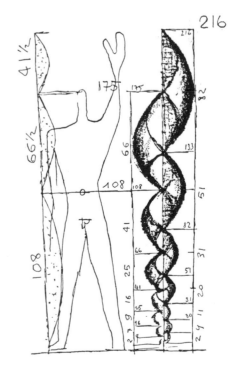

73 Le Corbusier, op. cit., Part III: 'Il s'agit, en fait, de transformer radicalement de contrition en joie vaillante, ce temps de la vie qui en est le plus long!'
74 Le Corbusier, op. cit., Part IV. Réalités, I. De l'Océan à l'Oural. 'Elément constitutif – et des plus essentiels – du futur statut de monde, la cité linéaire des industries de transformation et d'achèvement est un thème naturellement destiné à une discussion internationale autour d'un tapis vert.'

question to a common denominator: man'.[75] It is significant that at the time he was collecting together in *The Modulor* the results of many years' study, a proportional scale based on human stature, to be used as a guide-line at the planning stage. Although inspired by the principles of the golden section, immutably defined as the 'fundamental expression of a unitary universe . . . a cardinal point of reference, echoing and re-echoed in all things from the smallest to the largest, and harmonising each separate part with the whole',[76] Le Corbusier's *modulor*, taken as a *grille de proportion*, cannot be considered a passive, scholarly revival of classicism. Nor is it an approach imitating the speculation of Renaissance theory. The latter imposed, dogmatically, through determinations made possible by the study of perspective, numbers and ratios for the anthropometric definition of architecture in order to make the proportions of man a universal point of reference and answer in figurative terms the philosophical premises of the time.

In fact nothing lends itself more significantly and obviously to the purpose of universal harmony than the human figure inscribed in the perfect limits of circle and square.[77] Man as an exceptional, autonomous and perfect individual therefore represented, in his static geometry the centre of the universe, and his symmetry and proportion become synonymous with unity and the guarantee of harmonious reference. However, Le Corbusier's man is not an archaeological imitation of the *homo ad quadratum* and *ad circulum* isolated in the geometric microcosm of a simple, flat figure. He is a united and dynamic man, a unit consciously related to the whole and to the environment.

It is this continuous and active contact with the totality of the system which reveals the need for a rationalisation of relations. In other words it demands a dimensional truth which takes into account human use of things, human movements in space assumed at the moment of use, and the economy of those movements. Le Corbusier's man, understood as a biological organism and thus subject to the laws of birth, growth, flowering and decay, is a radical change from the axiomatic idea of man in his invariable perfection. Having discarded all symbolic and contemplative significance and revived and revalued man's function, one can replace the possible modular interpretations in a more substantial environment.

The *modulor* is no longer 'an abstract measure of absolute and invariable beauty, but a measure equated with a certain man who carries out certain basic functions in the world around him. It is a projection of the idea of man and his activities, which articulates them in numerical terms to maintain the expansion of his psychic and physical organism in basic agreement with a world which is no longer external, but suitably adapted and humanised. Again it is not based on aesthetic values but includes a fuller and more varied scale of components; it consolidates a drama of action and potential and, in the man–nature relationship, is more complex and vigorous; nothing would emerge from the inertia of unchanging contemplation.'[78] It will therefore come as no surprise that the scheme of subtle mathematical connections, derived from the basic measure of the modulor-man,[79] is the very axis of the aggressive reality of *l'Unité d'habitation* of Marseilles.

When *l'Unité d'habitation* and its unprecedented forms became an integral part of the Marseilles landscape, the cycle of the 'town-planning revolution'

75 Le Corbusier, *Manière de Penser l'Urbanisme*. Chapter V. *Les Règles: Humain et Nature*. 'Pour juger des réponses à donner aux formidables questions posées par l'époque et concernant son équipement, une seule mesure est admissible qui ramènera toute question aux bases mêmes: l'humain.'
76 G. Kopes, *Modularita in natura e in arte* in *Casabella*, No. 307, July, 1966.
77 For symbolism connected with the human figure inscribed in a circle see R. Wittkower, *Principi architettonici nell'età dell'Umanesimo*. Einaudi, Turin, 1964.
78 C. L. Ragghianti, op. cit.
79 Le Corbusier defines the Modulor as a 'range of harmonious measurements to suit the human scale, universally applicable to architecture and to mechanical things'. The Modulor is a system of measurement based on the stature of man with his arm upraised (226 cm.), which gives an unlimited series of related proportions. For example 226 cm. = $113 + 70 \times 43$ cm.; 113, 70 and 43 are measurements based on the Golden Sections and fit many characteristic positions of the human body in space. A seated man corresponds to 43 cm., a man leaning at a table to 70 cm., or against a parapet, 113 cm.: or else $113 + 70 = 183$ cm. = man's average height. For a more thorough study of the subject refer to the two volumes by Le Corbusier: *Le Modulor* and *Modulor 2*.

17 *L'Unité d'habitation*, Marseilles.
Detail of the external side
staircase

was coming full circle. The social and political ideal of all-embracing harmony *('Grande Harmonie')*, put forward by Fourier in his 'Phalanstery'
project,[80] pursued for more than a century, then taken up on several occasions by Le Corbusier, became a working reality, or as Giedion says 'social
imagination' finally achieved 'three-dimensional expression'.[81]

L'Unité of Marseilles was the sum of previous hypotheses and experiments,
and, above all, at that time a triumph over the architectural hypocrisies
which, in the name of the need for rebuilding, were blanketing whole areas
of the centres and suburbs of European cities, like some inferior quality
ground-covering.

The unashamed practicality of *l'Unité* proved annoying to the undis-
criminating and provincial conservativism of the *Société pour l'Esthétique de
la France* as it did to those prejudiced critics who could not see Le Corbusier's
logical creative continuity in the free plastic forms, and were quick to
denounce them as open repudiation of rationalist sanctions. They little
imagined that they were soon to see their monotonous criticism radically
upset by the overwhelming experience of Ronchamp.

Just as *l'Unité* met with aesthetic judgements of form, so it came up against
Francastel's negative socio-functional evaluation.[82] He considered that the
complex internal arrangement of dwellings and common services lessened
the degree of human freedom. In fact, this dangerous critical attitude is

80 Charles Fourier, *Traité de l'Association domestique-agricole,* Paris, 1841.
81 S. Giedion, *Space, Time and Architecture,* Part IV. *Le Corbusier between 1938 and 1952.*
82 Pierre Francastel, *L'arte e la civiltà moderna,* Milan, 1959.

quashed once one recognises that *l'Unité d'habitation* is the intermediate link in the theoretical chain which, as we have seen, was initially intended to tackle the main themes of town-planning, starting by solving the problem of the living-cell. The shades of Utopia pale before such persistent and consistent proposals and any extremes, due to early ambitions, are eventually resolved as the overall design progresses. This design is controlled by the conviction of being the instrument of a transformation restricted only by society's limits of acceptance. One ought to remember that for many of Le Corbusier's contemporaries the passage between formulation and realisation was a fatal labyrinth in which they became irremediably lost.

Le Corbusier did not lose his way, on the contrary, *l'Unité* at Marseilles strengthened his dogged faith in his own creed. He felt that here at last was proof of his basic arguments and, having obtained such proof, he could confront new hypotheses, confident of further positive results. He could now dedicate himself completely to developing the theme which had remained in a state of latent potential because other objectives, more important at the time, had had to be fulfilled first. All the plastic energy, which for so long had been restricted by the dominance of rationalist thought, now burst forth with the impetus of liberation, accentuated by the flattery of the landscape in the '*espace indicible*' of Ronchamp. His final phase opens with and is characterised by Ronchamp; it was his most creative work in which many have wanted to find elements which betray an ideal or show a lapse of consistency.

But degeneration and survival do not feature in Le Corbusier's vocabulary, unlike other European masters of modern architecture; he is immune from that characteristic phenomenon of acquiescence which reduces *avant-garde*

19 *L'Unité d'habitation*,
Nantes-Rezé

20 *L'Unité d'habitation*,
Nantes-Rezé. Representation
of the Modulor in the cement
of the façade

'hopes' to the 'certainties' of a social and cultural conservativism altogether foreign to him. Le Corbusier was always the standard-bearer of anti-conformity, consistency and courage. To the very last he remained the leading protagonist through his inexhaustible wealth of inventiveness, seen in his continuous experiments, the constant achievement of his own aims and that 'heretical habit, driving-force of all his artistic desires'.[83]

The architecture of Ronchamp seems to the author to be proof of a continuity of patient research, and above all of a plastic vocation.[84] From his very earliest works, even the most stereometrical, the very severe structural arrangement is always softened by a lyrical vein in the contrasting plastic forms. One cannot deny that the roof-top of the Villa Savoye already has latent in it the first and not so timid plastic-formal 'turbulences'.

There are those who disregard the well-spaced, consistent progression which leads to the remarkable figurative results of the *Plan-obus* and *l'Unité* at Marseilles and consider these plastic tendencies destructive manifestations of manneristic formalism, superimposed on the context as though they were the outcome of a second, distracted moment of creation. Such theses seem false arguments since one must remember the way in which Le Corbusier with equal intensity, had developed and elaborated formal themes alongside similar lines in both painting and sculpture. This was an extension of his search for interconnecting and modulated relationships. The architecture of Ronchamp might be interpreted as the dominance and elevation of only one of the components which normally exist in Le Corbusier's poetry.

83 B. Zevi, *Ricordo di Le Corbusier*, in *Ideal Standard*, July–November, 1965.
84 For a fuller discussion of this conviction see author's *La Capella di Ronchamp. Forma e colore*, *No. 58*, Sadea Sansoni, Florence, 1968.

However, this would not mean that the impetus towards plasticity finally destroyed or excluded the tight-knit background provided by a guiding rational process.

While form, as the result of method, becomes an important theme in his later works, it never has a moralising or pedagogic purpose, nor is it ever intended to show off anything which is not strictly in accord with human and natural situations and it is never there just for the sake of style. Form is felt as essential movement, thought of as an active element of synthesis and a natural echo of temporal conditions, in the basic conviction that architecture is realised and brought to life only by being given shape and form.

Form was thus a theme which Le Corbusier pursued for a long time and finally achieved in his mature works. In the same way, light was another basic component of his architecture, which was used continuously but only exploited to the full in the buildings after Ronchamp.

The building of the monastery of La Tourette (1959) dispelled any reservations that there may still have been about the validity of Ronchamp. What is more, the evident methodical continuity of spatial hypotheses, based on the same spiritual yardstick, proved that the hasty judgement of Ronchamp as a superfluous anomaly in the body of Le Corbusier's work was mistaken. There is in the Dominican monastery, as at Ronchamp, the eloquence of a formal vocabulary punctuating the assertion of dynamic space, but it is perhaps more constricted and subdued in its expression. There is the same tension between the interior and exterior which, in the area circumscribed by the courtyard-cloister, crystallises in dialectical exchanges round the corridors connecting the two adjacent physical realities. There is also the same use of light, which, filtering through openings that are bolder and more varied in shape, gives new stimulus and life to the elements of the internal spatial interaction in the church. It is the light factor which regulates

21 to 25 (on the preceding pages and opposite above). Chandigarh, The Legislative Assembly, general view, and details showing the façade, portico, the side elevation and vestibule

26 (opposite, below). Chandigarh, The Secretariat

27 Chandigarh, The Secretariat. Detail of the *brise-soleil*

28 Chandigarh, The Secretariat. Detail of the roof and amenities

From La Tourette to Chandigarh

Pls. 21 to 26, Fig. 18

29 Sketch for the monument of the Open Hand at Chandigarh

30 Sketch for the parish church at Firminy

the levels of the graduated series of altars reserved for common worship and enlivens the functional monotony of the passages, welcoming and exalting the act of procession. Light gives rhythm to the chaste silence of the refectory without undermining respect for a fundamental rule of the order.

Finally, the selection and treatment of building materials was obviously made in order to achieve an integration with the authentic natural elements of the site. These observations on the relationships between light and form as catalysing elements of space and as points of contact in the placing of free forms can be applied to the buildings of Chandigarh, or of Ahmedabad.

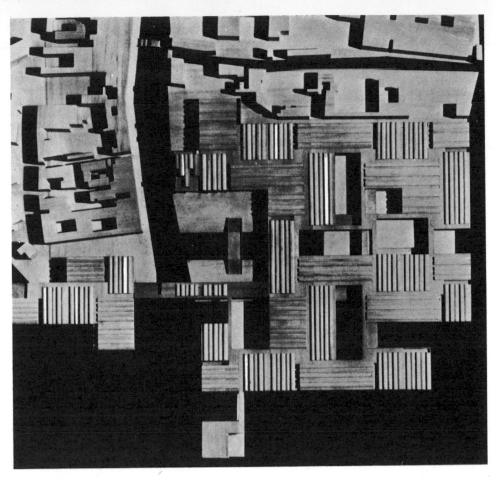

They can be expanded with reference to other features because of the special
climatic conditions and the primitive expressiveness that the material acquires
through rudimentary working.

The great constructions at Chandigarh provide emphatic proof of how
much and how sensitively Le Corbusier had to adapt to the pressures inherent
in the commission. When asked by the government of the Punjab to furnish
a town-planning scheme for the new capital, Le Corbusier saw the opportunity for creating the whole appearance of a new city, situated in an
environment with specific climatic conditions, which had no previous
historical existence and was in sight of a singularly striking and suggestive
landscape. The temptation to invent a new urban form was perhaps his first
reaction to the inspiring task, but the fear of rejection of yet another proposal
for a structure ahead of its time led him to choose the solution of an acceptable
town-planning scheme along the lines advocated in *La Charte d'Athènes* and
Les Trois Etablissements Humains and to concentrate his powerful inventive   Pls. 31 to 38, Figs. 21 to 28
ambition on building the Capitol. He realised that the time had come to
abandon experiment and seize an opportunity of leaving effective proof of
his talents. He felt that he did not have as much time ahead of him as he
wanted and that he had to take the safe path. This decision did not mean complete surrender, but more of a flexible attitude to the problems of a society
which springs from a moral, social and psychological tradition remote from
Western society which is committed to strive for greater equality and
innovation.

Within the symbolistic structure of this newly-founded city capital, and
with the classical pattern of a Capitol, Le Corbusier wanted to include the
Parliament building (or Legislative Assembly) the Secretariat and the High
Court. In order to do so without degenerating into the fatal mistake of
pompous rhetoric, and while maintaining a representative character on a
level which would not be in violent and artificial contrast to actual social
conditions, he created the device of featuring certain distinctive constituent
elements on a larger scale. With this revival, suggestive of the monumentality of a gigantic order, he obtained a structural support which allowed an
imposing free play of symmetries in depth, over which lay, on different

levels, the modulations of a cement grid, on a normal scale, which regulated ventilation and sunlight.

The visual interplay of the two orders creates an intentionally dramatic effect in the solemn chiaroscuro of the porticoes, vibrant with the changing lighting effect of reflections from the two mirrors of water. These designs achieve a moderated counterpoint to human stature, show a respect for humble social character, and follow the natural features of the site–positive qualities which distinguish Chandigarh from Brasilia, the other capital city founded during the fifties.[85]

Brasilia (1957) like Chandigarh (1951) was started on virgin soil, along the classical orthogonal lines of nineteenth-century capitals. However, the latter at the foot of the Himalayas managed to escape from customary limitations by force of genuine inspiration, while the scheme on the edge of the Mato Grosso became just another artificial repetition of a theoretical, formal pattern which has been imitated and transformed beyond recognition until it begins to be a dangerous, uncontrollable and destructive instrument.

Unlike Chandigarh, Brasilia, without doubt, set out to amaze and ended up with nothing but appearances, which easily change to nightmares. The Square of the Three Powers is a collection of ostentatious affectations: one can see in the hybrid arrangement of the strange shapes of inhuman and rhetorical buildings the theatrical excesses of an over-enthusiastic political class, a hasty cover-up of profound social contrasts and a regurgitation of all nationalistic ambitions.

Fig. 31

Even with its shortcomings, therefore, Chandigarh is a lesson in moderation and as such, like his last project for the Venice hospital, an occasion for hope for a man still in command of, and aware of the importance and quality of his works.

The man for whom Le Corbusier created his work is perhaps the last 'free man', the one who refuses to be reduced to the level of a unit in a consumer society, who does not want to be employed anonymously alongside a machine, who wants to avoid the conditioning caused by the pathological disturbances of the modern city.

Against the backdrop of a historical period in which compromise has become systematic and accepted, Le Corbusier personifies the man who has always refused to recognise 'easy' standpoints, who has uncovered the political masquerades which appear to support culture but which are really trying to adapt its power to its own uses. He has steadfastly sought for a formula to set to rights the chaos of an era, and come forward with the suggestion that in order to give any meaning to architecture in the context of contemporary society, the constant, fervent striving for a way to help maintain human equilibrium must ultimately be resolved by an act of faith. Planning, apart from forcing recognition of the uncertainty of situations, must be creative and constructive, an instrument of communication. Only then will it have any value as an example, a point of reference, which has a moral and material lesson.

The work of Le Corbusier has many aspects and can be interpreted in many ways. With a careful analysis of the successive stages of its development, and by contrast and comparison, we have sought to show in this survey how Le Corbusier's prolific and creative vitality has always gone hand in hand with a persuasive logic, capable of enforcing his new ideas. For these he has been labelled the 'difficult genius of architecture', but with his basic method of *'recherche patiente'* he established once and for all the form and history of *'l'esprit nouveau'* of our time.

---

85 With the aim of moving part of the social and economic activity from the Atlantic coast, it was decided in 1955, on the initiative of J. Kubitschek, to transfer the political capital to the interior. Thus started the 'Brasilia' adventure. The Brazilian architect Niemeyer was commissioned to design several buildings, among which was the President's residence. Only later in March 1957, at Niemeyer's own suggestion was a competition arranged (with a six month deadline) for the city-planning scheme. Lucio Costa, another Brazilian architect, was the prizewinner with his scheme in the shape of an aeroplane. The buildings of the Square of the Three Powers were constructed from designs by Niemeyer.

2

4

6

8

10

14

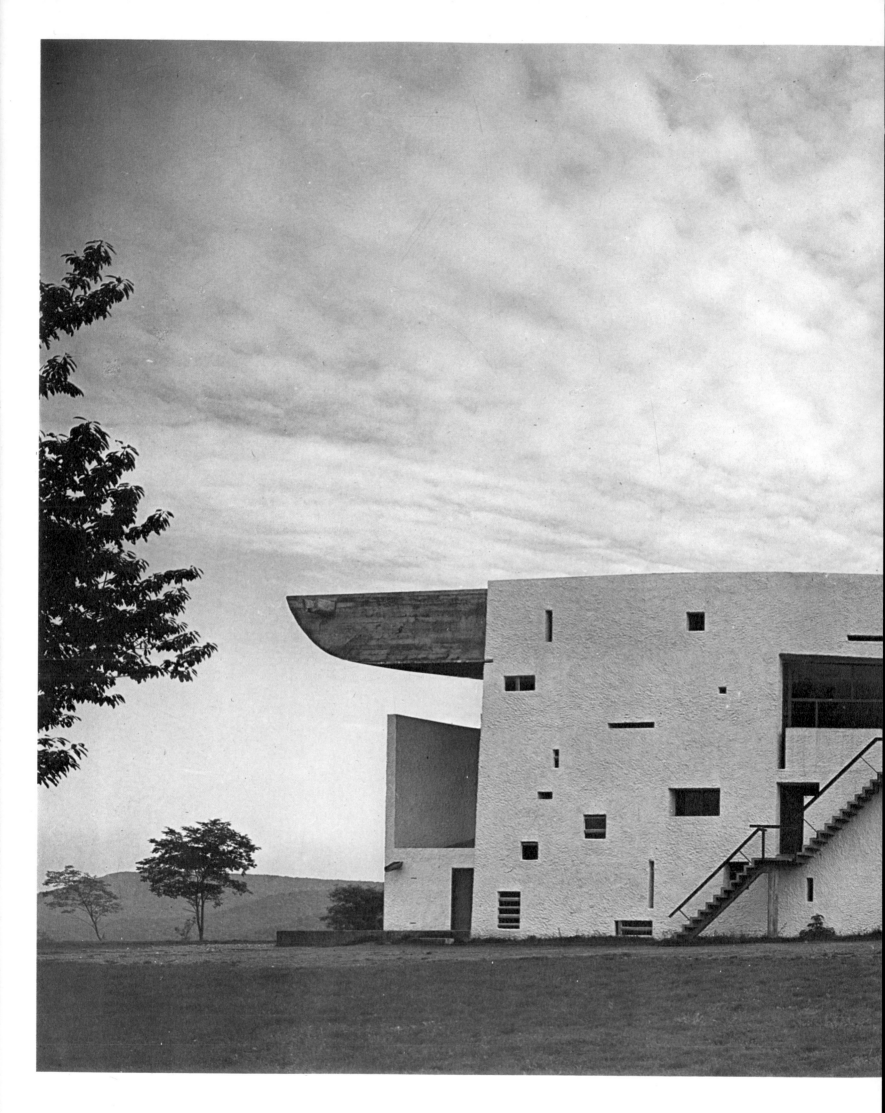

21

22

23

27

28

29

31

32

33

34

35

36

37

38

39

40

44

Description of colour plates

1 Garches, Villa Stein
The main elevation seen from the road

2 Garches, Villa Stein
View of the rear elevation

3 Garches, Villa Stein
Detail of the rear elevation

4 Poissy, Villa Savoye
General view

5 Poissy, Villa Savoye
Corner view

6 Poissy, Villa Savoye

7 Poissy, Villa Savoye
Detail of the inside staircase

8 Paris, *Cité universitaire,* Swiss pavilion

9 Marseilles, *Unité d'habitation*
Detail of the façade

10 Marseilles, *Unité d'habitation*
Detail of the school on the roof-terrace

11 Marseilles, *Unité d'habitation*
Detail of ventilation chimney

12 Ronchamp, Chapel of Notre Dame du Haut
General view from the south-east

13 Ronchamp, Chapel of Notre Dame du Haut
South façade

14 Ronchamp, Chapel of Notre Dame du Haut
Looking north towards the outside pulpit

15 Ronchamp, Chapel of Notre Dame du Haut
The north wall showing the stairway leading to the sacristy
and the two bell-towers

16 Ronchamp, Chapel of Notre Dame du Haut
View from the north-west

17 Ronchamp, Chapel of Notre Dame du Haut
South wall, external view of the processional entrance

18–19 Ronchamp, Chapel of Notre Dame du Haut
View of the north façade;
the smaller bell-towers mark the secondary entrance

20 Ronchamp, Chapel of Notre Dame du Haut
Interior view looking south

21 Monastery of Ste-Marie de la Tourette
View of the north and west façades

22 Monastery of Ste-Marie de la Tourette
View of the south façade

23 Monastery of Ste-Marie de la Tourette
Detail of the north façade showing the 'light cannons'

24 Monastery of Ste-Marie de la Tourette
Detail of internal courtyard

25 Monastery of Ste-Marie de la Tourette
Detail of internal courtyard

26 Monastery of Ste-Marie de la Tourette
Detail of the light cannons

27 Nantes-Rezé, *Unité d'habitation*
General view

28 Nantes-Rezé, *Unité d'habitation*
Detail of the reliefs on the façade

29 Nantes-Rezé, *Unité d'habitation*
Detail of the *pilotis*

30 Nantes-Rezé, *Unité d'habitation*
Roof terrace, showing part of a covered way

31 Chandigarh, The High Court of Justice

32 Chandigarh, The Legislative Assembly

33 Chandigarh, The Legislative Assembly

34 Chandigarh. In the foreground the portico
of the Legislative Assembly, behind it the Secretariat

35, 36 Chandigarh, The Secretariat
Details of the main façade, showing ramp

37 Chandigarh, The Secretariat
Detail of the façade showing the *brise-soleil* (sun-breakers)
of the minister's offices

38 Chandigarh, View of Assembly roof
from the terrace of the High Court

39 Ahmedabad
Detail of the building of the Weaver's Association

40 Ahmedabad, Museum
General view

41 Cambridge (Massachusetts), Visual Arts Center
View of the east façade and access ramp

42 Firminy, Youth and cultural centre
View of the west façade

43 Firminy, Youth and cultural centre
Detail of the west bridge

44 Firminy, Youth and cultural centre
Detail of south wall showing reliefs

45 Firminy, Youth and cultural centre
Detail of the west façade

46 Firminy, Youth and cultural centre
View of the west façade

Biographical notes

Charles Edouard Jeanneret, the future Le Corbusier, was born at La Chaux-de-Fonds, in the Jura, on October 6th, 1887. His father was an engraver of watch-cases and his mother Maria Charlotte Amelie Perret was a musician.

At the age of fourteen he went to the École d'Art of La Chaux-de-Fonds, where he did his apprenticeship as engraver and chiseller. Under Charles L'Eplattenier he studied from nature and had his first instruction in the history of art.

In 1902 he executed the engraving for a watch which was exhibited and awarded a diploma at the International Exhibition of the Decorative Arts in Turin. In 1905 he built his first house at La Chaux-de-Fonds for one of the school administrators.

In 1906 on the advice of L'Eplattenier, who was encouraging him to take up architecture, he went to Italy; he visited Florence, Siena and Pisa. The following year he went to Vienna where he frequented Josef Hoffmann's studio, but he was attracted by Loos and his anti-conformism. In February, 1908, he arrived in Paris and was employed in Auguste Perret's studio where he learnt the importance of building in reinforced concrete.

In 1910 he retired with his text-books to the mountains to study the calculations of reinforced concrete. Later he went to Peter Behrens's studio in Berlin where he met Mies van der Rohe and Walter Gropius. From Behrens he learnt to appreciate clarity of conceptual lay-out, how to tackle and resolve the relationships between design and industry and envisage possibilities for future development in architecture.

In 1911 and 1912 he visited the Balkans, Greece and Asia Minor. On his return from this study tour, he came into contact with various currents of the European *avant-garde* and chose to turn towards rationalism. During this phase he worked out the elements of his architecture which are clearly outlined in the project for the Dom-Ino house. At the outbreak of the First World War he went back to teach at La Chaux-de-Fonds.

In 1917 he returned to Paris to live, and became a close friend of the painter Amédée Ozenfant. His association and collaboration with Ozenfant resulted, a year later, in the manifesto *Après le Cubisme* which was the act of foundation of the Purist movement. His first painting experiments date from this period. In 1920, again with Ozenfant, and with the poet Paul Dermée, he founded *L'Esprit Nouveau,* an international review of aesthetics.

From 1920 to 1922 he worked on the project for the Citrohan house and launched the formula of the *machine à habiter*.

In 1921 with his cousin Pierre Jeanneret he started the studio at 35, rue de Sèvres where he worked until 1965.

The plan for a 'contemporary city for three million inhabitants' which was exhibited at the Paris *Salon d'Automne,* dates from 1922 and at the same time he designed and built a studio house for Ozenfant and a villa at Vaucresson.

1923 saw the publication in *L'Esprit Nouveau* of articles which formed a substantial part of one of his most famous publications; *Vers une Architecture.*

The project for the Roche-Jeanneret house in Paris dates from this period as does the publication of the last number of the review *L'Esprit Nouveau,* number 28, and his study for the *immeubles-villas* projects. On the occasion of the International Exhibition of Decorative Arts in Paris in 1925 he built for the pavilion of *L'Esprit Nouveau* a prototype of one of the living cells of the *immeubles-villas* and in it exhibited his *Plan Voisin* for Paris. (The plan was given the name of the industrialist, a manufacturer of cars and aeroplanes, whose financial backing made possible the construction of the pavilion.) Using ideas from his experiments for the Citrohan houses, he planned and built at Pessac, Bordeaux, a housing estate which met with hostile reactions from official critics and the administrative bureaucracy.

1927 was the year of two events of fundamental importance, the building, following the strict rules of the *'tracés régulateurs',* of the Villa Stein at Garches, and the study for the project submitted for the competition for the Palace of the League of Nations in Geneva. Official hypocrisy after a second competition preferred to entrust the task to four architects exhibiting in the prevailing academic vein. (In the first competition Le Corbusier's project had been eliminated because it was not drawn in Indian ink.)

For the experimental *Weissenhof* quarter in Stuttgart, he planned and built two buildings which exemplify the concepts drawn up in his 'five points' of architecture. In the spring of 1928, in collaboration with Siegfried Giedion and the leading architects of the modern movement, he founded the C.I.A.M. *(Congrès International d'Architecture Moderne)* to defend the cause of modern architecture.

The Villa Savoye, designed in 1928 and finished in 1930, is the most pure and consistent embodiment of the planning ideas of the rationalist vocabulary.

1928 was the year when Le Corbusier turned his hand to designing a number of pieces of furniture, among which the most famous were the *chaise-longue* and two armchairs which only went into mass-production in 1965.

That same year he started the plans for the commission from the Government of the U.S.S.R. for the Palace of the Union of the Co-operatives (Centrosoyus) in Moscow.

32 Le Corbusier in his studio

During a lecture tour in South America in 1929, he became aware of the problems of the increase in size of the cities of Rio de Janeiro, São Paulo, Montevideo and Buenos Aires, and put forward highly original suggestions for town-planning schemes to solve them.

The first draft of the study for the replanning of the city of Algiers dates from 1930 as does the project (executed later) for the Swiss pavilion in the *cité universitaire* in Paris.

Another major event occupied the activity of the studio in rue de Sèvres in 1931: the competition for the Palace of the Soviets in Moscow. The result was yet another profound disillusionment, the Russian, Jofan, won with a project which was completely in line with the most antiquated monumentality.

Meanwhile the first stage of the project for a 'growing' museum was started which was later elaborated in several stages.

Between 1932 and 1933 he designed and built the Salvation Army hostel in Paris, putting into practice his first attempt at an air-conditioning plant to regulate thermal reflections in the interior by the adoption of a façade of a wall of fixed glass.

In 1932 he built the Clarté block in Geneva which had the first duplex apartment.

Studies for the Durand lots, and an apartment block in Algiers (use of the *brise-soleil*) were in hand in 1933–4 as was the project for the Retenanstalt offices in Zurich and the construction of an apartment building at Porte Molitor where Le Corbusier took a flat himself. The project for *la ville radieuse* (the radial city) published in 1938, and the town-planning scheme for Nemours (Algeria) date from 1934.

In autumn, 1935, he was invited to hold a series of lectures in the United States. He started the controversy on the skyscrapers of New York, which he resumed on his return to Europe in the book *Quand les cathédrales étaient blanches. Voyage au pays des timides*. He built a little holiday house on the outskirts of Paris and another at Mathes.

In 1936 he was summoned by Lucio Costa to advise on council for the project for the New Ministry of Education and Public Health in Rio de Janeiro and flew there in a Graf-Zeppelin airship. He advised the use of a *brise-soleil* to minimise the effect of the sun's rays on the façade of the building

Meanwhile he was still making suggestions for town-planning schemes to improve Paris and projected a stadium for 100,000 spectators. For the 1937 International Exhibition in Paris he erected the *Pavillon des Temps Nouveaux*.

He designed the monument to the memory of Deputy Vaillant

33 Le Corbusier

Couturier, where for the first time he used the symbol of a large open hand which he employed later at Chandigarh.

The project for the Cartesian skyscraper and the plan for Buenos Aires both date from 1938.

From 1939 he was unable to operate because of the war. During the war years he published *La Charte d'Athènes* with Jean Giraudoux's introduction in 1941 and *Les Trois Establissements Humains* in 1944. He also continued his work on the projects for the plan of Algiers.

At the end of the war (1945), he resumed his studies of *'tracés regulateurs'* and brought them to a conclusion. After these he went on to propose the Modulor, measurement based on human stature.

He continued with his plans for the reconstruction of Saint-Dié, which was to become the prototype for international post-war town-planning, and for the *l'Unité d'habitation* of Marseilles. Although the plan for Saint-Dié never progressed further than the drawing-board, the Marseilles *Unité*, despite a thousand difficulties and oppositions, was finally built thanks to the decisiveness of Claudius Petit who was then Minister for Reconstruction; it was inaugurated in 1953.

In 1947, as a member of the International Commission formed to study the project for the headquarters of the U.N., he put forward the basic ideas for the eventual realisation of the complex but was dismissed before it was built.

Between 1946 and 1950 he designed a housing complex for Cap Martin, the C.I.A.M. grid, an underground church for Saint-Baume, city plans for La Rochelle and Bogotà and built an industrial building in Saint-Dié. In 1950 the Chapel at Ronchamp marked the beginning of the last phase of his work. At long last the projects carried through outnumbered those left on the drawing-board.

From 1952 to 1960 he built *l'Unité d'habitation* at Nantes and one in Berlin, the Dominican monastery of La Tourette, the Phillips pavilion at the Brussels World Fair, a museum, the building for the Weavers Association, various villas at Ahmedabad in India and a museum in Tokyo.

From 1951 he was chiefly occupied with the preparation of plans and projects for the great capital city of the Punjab. Not only did he provide the whole overall plan for Chandigarh (the fortress of the god Chandi) but between 1956 and 1965 he built all the buildings of the Capitol complex.

From 1961 to 1965 he designed the French embassy in Brasilia, a Congress Hall in Strasbourg, an Electronic Calculation Centre for Olivetti at Rho-Milan, a church for Firminy and his only work in the United States, the Visual Arts Center at Cambridge, Massachusetts.

He died of a heart attack while swimming in the sea off Cap Martin on August 27th, 1965, aged 78.

Catalogue of buildings

1905 House at La Chaux-de-Fonds.

1922 Villa at Vaucresson. Ozenfant's studio in Paris.

1923 The La Roche-Jeanneret House.

1924 Studio for Lipschitz at Boulogne-sur-Seine.

1925 Little house on Lac Léman. Housing at Pessac, Bordeaux. Pavilion of *L'Esprit Nouveau*, at the *Exposition d'arts décoratifs* in Paris.

1926 Studio for an artist at Boulogne-sur-Seine. *Palais du Peuple* (for the Salvation Army) in Paris. *Fondation de Polignac*, Paris. The Cook House at Boulogne-sur-Seine. House Guiette, Antwerp.

1927 Villa Stein at Garches. Two houses for Weissenhof, Stuttgart. Planeix house in Paris.

1928–9 Restaurant at Ville d'Avray.

1928 Nestlé pavilion.

1929–31 Villa Savoye, Poissy. Floating shelter for the Salvation Army, Paris.

1929–33 Palace of Centrosoyus at Moscow.

1930 House Erraguriz, Chili.

1930–1 Champs Elysées apartment, Paris. The De Mandrot Villa at Le Pradet, Toulon.

1930–2 Clarté apartment building in Geneva. Swiss pavilion in the *cité universitaire* of Paris.

1932–3 Hostel for the Salvation Army in Paris.

1933 Apartment building at Porte Molitor, Paris.

1935 Week-end house in the suburbs of Paris. Summer house at Mathes.

1936–45 Ministry of Education and Public Health in Rio de Janeiro (in collaboration with Lucio Costa and Oscar Niemeyer).

1937 Pavilion of Modern Times at the Paris International Exhibition of Art and Industry.

1946–51 Duval factory at Saint-Dié.

1947–52 *L'Unité d'habitation* at Marseilles.

1949 Currutchet House at La Plata.

1950–4 Chapel of Notre Dame du Haut at Ronchamp.

1952 Summer house at Cap Martin.

1952–7 *L'Unité d'habitation* at Nantes-Rezé.

1954–6 Villa Sarabhai at Ahmedabad. Villa Shodan at Ahmedabad.

1955–7 Jaoul house at Neuilly-sur-Seine.

1956–7 *L'Unité d'habitation* at Berlin. Building for the Association of Weavers at Ahmedabad. Museum at Ahmedabad.

1956–65 High Court at Chandigarh. Secretariat at Chandigarh. Legislative Assembly at Chandigarh.

1957–9 Brazilian pavilion in the *cité universitaire*, Paris (in collaboration with Lucio Costa).

1957–9 Museum in Tokyo.

1957–9 *L'Unité d'habitation* at Briey-en-Foret. Monastery of Ste-Marie de la Tourette at Eveux, Lyons.

1958 Phillips pavilion at the World Fair, Brussels.

1961–4 Visual Arts Center at Cambridge (Massachusetts).

1961–5 Youth and cultural centre, Firminy.

1964–5 An exhibition pavilion at Zurich.

Paintings by Le Corbusier

34 *Still-life*, 1923
Museum of Modern Art, Paris

35 *Vertical guitar*, 1953
Museum of Modern Art, Paris

36 *Taureau VI*, 1954
Museum of Modern Art, Paris

Bibliography

S. GIEDION, *Le Corbusier et l'architecture contemporaine, Cahiers d'Art*, V, Paris, 1930; F. DE PIERREFEU, *Le Corbusier et P. Jeanneret*, Paris, 1932; *L'architecture d'aujourd'hui*, IV, 10, 1933, 38, 1948 (Special Nos.); A. ROTH, *Zwei Häuser in Stuttgart*, Stuttgart, 1934; L. MUMFORD, *The Culture of Cities*, New York, 1938; J. M. RICHARDS, *An Introduction to Modern Architecture*, Harmondsworth, 1940 (3rd ed. 1957); S. GIEDION, *Space, Time and Architecture*, Cambridge (Mass.), 1944 (3rd ed. 1956); M. GAUTHIER, *Le Corbusier ou l'architecture au service de l'homme*, Paris, 1944; *Unité d'habitation à Marseille de Le Corbusier, L'homme et l'architecture*, 11–14, 1947 (Special No.); S. PAPADAKI (ed.), *Le Corbusier; Architect, Painter, Writer*, New York, 1948; J. ALAZARD, *Le Corbusier*, Florence, Paris, 1950 (Eng. trans. New York 1960); *L'Unité d'habitation de Marseille* (Point 38), Mulhouse, 1950 (Eng. trans., G. Sainsbury, *The Marseilles Block*, London, 1953); B. ZEVI, *Storia dell'architettura moderna*, Turin, 1950; A. GATTI, *L'abitazione nell'architettura di Le Corbusier*, Rome, 1953; *Architecture du bonheur, Forces Vives*, 5–7, 1955 (Special No.); *Les Chapelles du Rosaire à Vence par Henri Matisse et de Notre Dame du Haut à Ronchamp par Le Corbusier* (*L'art sacré*, 1–2 Special No.), Paris, 1955; E. M. FRY, *Chandigarh: New Capital City, Architectural Record*, CXVII, 1955; E. N. ROGERS, *Il metodo di Le Corbusier, e la forma nella 'Chapelle de Ronchamp', Casabella*, 207, 1955; A. E. BRINCKMANN, *Baukunst*, Tübingen, 1956; *Chandigarh: Le Corbusier architecte, Aujourd'hui*, VII, 1956; *Construction en pays chauds: Chandigarh, Architecture d'aujourd'hui*, XXVII, 66, 1956; P. FRANCASTEL, *Art et technique*, Paris, 1956; S. GIEDION, *Architektur und Gemeinschaft, Tagebuch einer Entwicklung*, Hamburg, 1956 (Eng. trans., J. Tyrwhitt, *Architecture, You and Me*, Cambridge, Mass., 1958); A. HENZE, *Ronchamp*, Recklinghausen, 1956; G. SAMONÀ, *Lettura della cappella à Ronchamp, L'Architettura II*, 1956; H. BAUR, *Ronchamp und die neuere kirchliche Architektur Werk*, 44, 1957; N. PEVSNER, *Outline of European Architecture*, London, 1957; A. HENZE, *Le Corbusier*, Berlin, 1957; *Kunsthaus, Le Corbusier* (cat.), Zurich, 1957 (bibliog.); *Le Corbusier: Chapelle Notre-Dame du Haut de Ronchamp, Cahiers Forces Vives*, Paris, 1957; *Unité d'habitation in Nantes-Rezé, Bauen und Wohnen*, XII, 1957; H. PERRUCHOT, *Le Corbusier*, Paris, 1958; F. FRICKER, *Le Corbusier: la Tourette, convento domenicano a Eveux, Architettura Cantiere*, 22, 1959; J. PETIT, *Le Corbusier propose: des unités d'habitation 1960 en séries, Zodiac*, 7, 1960; P. BLAKE, *The Master Builders*, New York, 1960; W. BOESIGER and E. GIRSBERGER, *Le Corbusier*, Zurich, 1960; F. CHOAY, *Le Corbusier*, New York, 1960; J. ALAZARD and J. P. HEBERT, *De la fenêtre au pan de verre dans l'œuvre de Le Corbusier*, Paris, 1961; S. GIEDION, *Breviario di Architettura*, Milan, 1961; *Le Corbusier* (cat. Musée d'art moderne), Paris, 1962; V. SCULLY, *L'Architettura moderna*, Milan, 1963; HENZE—MOOSBRUGGER, *La Tourette*, Starubery, 1963; H. RUSSELL HITCHCOCK, *Le Corbusier and the United States, Zodiac*, 16th July, 1966; S. GIEDION, *The Carpenter Center for Visual Arts* (Harvard University), *Zodiac*, 16th July, 1966; NORMA EVENSON, *Chandigarh*, University of California, 1966; W. BOESINGER—H. GIRSBERGER, *Le Corbusier, 1910–56*, Zurich, 1967; J. RIBOUD, *Les erreurs de Le Corbusier et leurs conséquences*, Paris, 1968; G. UNIACK, *De Vitruve à Le Corbusier*, Paris, 1968.

WRITINGS BY LE CORBUSIER

Étude sur le Mouvement d'Art décoratif en Allemagne, Haefli, La Chaux-de-Fonds, 1912; *Après le Cubisme* (in collaboration with A. Ozenfant), *Commentaires*, Paris, 1918; *Vers une Architecture, Collection de l'Esprit Nouveau*, Crès, Paris, 1923 (Eng. trans., F. Etchells, New York, 1927); *La Peinture Moderne* (in collaboration with A. Ozenfant), *Collection de l'Esprit Nouveau*, Crès, Paris, 1925; *L'Art décoratif d'aujourd'hui, Collection de l'Esprit Nouveau*, Crès, Paris, 1925 (2nd ed. 1959); *Urbanisme, Collection de l'Esprit Nouveau*, Paris, 1925 (Eng. trans., F. Etchells, *The City of Tomorrow and its Planning*, New York, 1929); *Almanach de l'Architecture moderne, Collection de l'Esprit Nouveau*, Crès, Paris, 1926; *Une Maison–Un Palais, Collection de l'Esprit Nouveau*, Crès, Paris, 1928; *Mundaneum* (in collaboration with P. Otlet), Brussels, 1928; *Précisions sur un état présent de l'Architecture et de l'Urbanisme, Collection de l'Esprit Nouveau*, Crès, Paris, 1930; *Croisade ou le Crépuscule des Académies, Collection de l'Esprit Nouveau*, Crès, Paris, 1923; *La Ville radieuse, Collection de l'Equipement de la Civilisation machiniste, L'Architecture d'aujourd'hui*, Paris, 1938; *Air Craft*, The New Vision Series, The Studio, London, 1935; *Quand les Cathédrales étaient blanches, Voyage au pays des timides*, Plon, Paris, 1937 (Eng. trans., F. E. Hyslop. *When Cathedrals were white. A journey to the country of timid people*. New York, 1947); *Des Canons. Des Munition? Merci! Des Logis . . . S.V.P., Collection de l'Equipement de la Civilisation machiniste, L'Architecture d'aujourd'hui*, Paris, 1938; *Le lyrisme des temps nouveaux et l'urbanisme*, Point, Colmar, 1939; *Destin de Paris, Collection Préludes*, Sorlot, Paris, 1941 (Eng. trans., D. Todd, London, 1947); *Sur les quatre routes, Collection de la Nouvelle Revue Française*, Gallimard, Paris, 1941; *Les Constructions 'Murondin'*, Chiron, Paris, 1941; *La maison des hommes* (in collaboration with F. de Pierrefeu), Plon, Paris, 1942 (Eng. trans., *The Home of Man*, London, 1948); *La Charte d'Athènes* (with a preface by J. Giraudoux, repr. Paris, 1957), Plon, Paris, 1943; *Entretien avec les étudiants des écoles d'architecture*, Denoël, Paris, 1943 (Eng. trans., P. Chase, New York, 1961); *Les trois établissements humains* (with others), Collection de l'Ascoral, Denoël, Paris, 1944; *Propos d'Urbanisme*, Bourrelier, Paris, 1946 (Eng. trans., C. Entwistle, *Concerning Town-planning*, London, 1947); *Manière de penser l'Urbanisme*, Collection de l'Ascoral, *L'Architecture d'aujourd'hui*, Paris, 1946; *Director plan for Buenos Aires*, 1947; *United Nations Headquarters*, Reinold, New York, 1947; *New World of Space*, New York, 1948 (Eng. trans., P. de Francia and A. Bostock, Cambridge, Mass., 1954); *Le Modular, Collection de l'Ascoral, l'Architecture d'aujourd'hui*, Boulogne-sur-Seine, 1949 (Eng. trans., P. de Francia and A. Bostock, Cambridge, Mass., 1954); *Poésie sur Alger*, Falaise, Paris, 1950; *L'Unité d'habitation de Marseille*, Point, Mulhouse, 1950; *Une petite Maison, Carnet de la recherche patiente*, Girsberger, Zurich, 1954; *Le Modulor II, Collection de l'Ascoral, L'Architecture d'aujourd'hui*, Boulogne-sur-Seine, 1955 (Eng. trans., P. de Francia and A. Bostock, Cambridge, Mass., 1958); *Le Poème de l'angle droit, Verve*, Paris, 1955; *Les Plans Le Corbusier pour Paris–1922–56*, Editions de Minuit, Paris, 1956; *La plus grande aventure du monde (l'architecture de Cîteaux)*, Grenoble, 1956; *Von der Poesie des Bauens* (selected texts), Zurich, 1957; *Ronchamp, Carnet de la recherche patiente*, Girsberger, Zurich, 1957 (Eng. trans., J. Cullen, *The Chapel at Ronchamp*, London, 1957); *Matisse, Léger, Le Corbusier; Moderne Kirchen* (selected texts), Zurich, 1958; *Le Poème électronique* (Pavillon Philips), Editions de Minuit, Paris, 1958; *L'Atelier de la recherche patiente*, Fréal, Paris, 1960 (Eng. trans. *Creation is a Patient Search*, trans., J. Palmes, New York, 1960; pub. as *My Work*, London, 1960); *L'urbanisme est une clé, Forces Vives*, Paris, 1966; *Œuvre Complète*, ed. W. Boesiger et al. (Eng. trans., P. Chase, New York, 1961), volume I, 1910–29; volume II, 1929–34; volume III, 1934–38; volume IV, 1938–46; volume V, 1946–52; volume VI, 1952–57; volume VII, 1957–65 (the first six vols. pub. by Girsberger, Zurich, the seventh by Les Editions d'Architecture, Zurich).